The Scottish Bed & Breakfast Book

The Scottish Bed & Breakfast Book

Country and Tourist Homes
Farms • Guesthouses • Inns

By June Skinner Sawyers

PELICAN PUBLISHING COMPANY
Gretna 2000

---

*The word "Pelican" and the depiction of a pelican are trademarks
of Pelican Publishing Company, Inc.,
and are registered in the U.S. Patent and Trademark Office.*

ISBN 1-56554-651-2

Illustrations and maps by Amelia Janes
Front cover: Schiehallion House (Grampian)

Information in this guidebook is based on authoritative data available at the time of printing. Prices listed are subject to change without notice. Readers are asked to take this into account when consulting this guide.

Manufactured in the United States of America

Published by Pelican Publishing Company, Inc.
1000 Burmaster Street, Gretna, Louisiana 70053

In memory of Bob Prentice,
perfect B&B host and
proud son of Scotland.

Contents

Introduction to Scotland

BACKGROUND

Scotland is one of the most beautiful countries in the world. As anyone who has traveled the many miles within its borders knows, Scotland is also a surprisingly diverse land, ranging from the gently rolling hills of the south to the wild and remote mountainous regions of the north. And yet all is not what it seems, for there are areas of the Lowlands that are much more hilly than what you may find in the Highlands. There's also something about the light and, in the Hebrides, the colors of the sea evoke more Mediterranean blues and greens than the cold waters of the northern isles. But then again Scotland is full of surprises.

At 30,414 square miles, Scotland is a small country—by American standards at least. But size can be deceiving. It's not as easy to get around as one might expect, for example. The roads, although mostly well traveled and relatively easy to navigate once you get the hang of it (which could take several days), nevertheless are smaller and much narrower than North American roads. You'll rarely find a multi-lane motorway in Scotland. On the contrary, the norm in this part of the world are two-lane roads and, in the more remote areas, single-track roads with traffic traveling in both directions (don't worry, passing places are strategically placed every 100 yards or so).

The cultural and historical highlights of Scotland are considerable. Edinburgh not only is the home to the world's largest arts festival, but also hosts one of the liveliest New Year celebrations. Meanwhile, Glasgow, not to be outshined, presents the increasingly popular Celtic Connections festival during the height of winter. (Glaswegians were never ones to allow little things like weather inconvenience them.) Among the newer attractions in Edinburgh surely the most significant must be the Museum of Scotland, which opened in late 1998, and tells the story of Scotland from prehistoric times to the present day. And anyone with even a passing interest in architecture must stop in Glasgow, the birthplace of Charles Rennie Mackintosh, that misunderstood and under-appreciated genius, as well as stomping grounds for countless unsung architects who plied their trade during the city's grand Victorian age.

Hence, unlike other B&B books, this guide is designed not only to help you find accommodations that best suit your tastes, but also to help you choose areas of the country that appeal to your specific interests. It also helps to know a little bit about a place before venturing into unfamiliar territory. If you want to bone up on your Scottish history and heritage (either in your native soil or while in Scotland itself), you might want to consider the following titles:

- *An Illustrated History of Scotland,* by Elisabeth Fraser (Norwich: Jarrold Publishing, 1997). A readable introduction to Scottish history, this work is profusely illustrated with archival photographs, drawings, and paintings.
- *Highlanders: A History of the Gaels,* by John Macleod (London: Sceptre, London, 1996). This is a compelling history of the Highlands by a popular journalist and fine stylist.
- *Hebridean Odyssey,* edited by Marion Sinclair (Edinburgh: Polygon, 1996). This collection celebrates the unique cultural heritage of the Hebrides in song, prose, poems, and images.
- *Consider the Lilies,* by Iain Crichton Smith (Edinburgh: Canongate, 1995). The Highland Clearances, the Scottish equivalent of the Irish Famine, are presented from the perspective of an old woman evicted from her home.

The Scottish Tourist Board has about 150 tourist information centers located in towns and villages throughout Scotland. The board also publishes several annual titles, including *Scotland: Bed & Breakfast,* with a listing of over 1,500 establishments (but no detailed descriptions). Other annually updated STB books include *Scotland: Hotels and Guest Houses, Scotland: Self-Catering,* and *Scotland: Camping & Caravan Parks.*

Information on travel in Scotland can be obtained from the following addresses:

Scottish Tourist Board
19 Cockspur Street
London SW1
Telephone: 0171-930-8661.

Scottish Tourist Board Central Information
23 Ravelston Terrace
Edinburgh
(Telephone and written inquiries only)
Telephone: 0131-332-2433
Fax: 0131-315-4545.

In the United States
British Tourist Authority
7th floor
551 Fifth Avenue
New York, NY 10176
1-800-GO2-BRITAIN.

British Tourist Authority
625 N. Michigan Avenue
Suite 1510
Chicago, IL 60611
Telephone: 1-800-462-2748.

In recent years the tourist board has been working diligently to not only aggressively encourage tourism to Scotland but also improve the quality of service, from B&Bs to restaurants and attractions. Thus, any establishment that displays the "Welcome Host" badge indicates that the staff has been trained to provide a higher caliber of service and hospitality. With a few exceptions, I have found this to be true.

The purpose of this book is to present to you descriptions of some of the best B&Bs in Scotland. They were chosen for ambiance, historic appeal, and period charm; sometimes because of their literary connections; and other times based on the warmth and personality of the owners themselves. For make no mistake about it, the B&B owner establishes the mood of the establishment. If they offer enthusiastic and genuine service, you, the guest, will be able to sense their caring attitude straightaway. On the other hand, if they project a suspicious or even hostile mood (and that has sometimes been the case), you'd best stay clear of them altogether.

One time I stayed at what seemed like a perfectly pleasant B&B from the outside, a handsome and charming townhouse that offered splendid views of the cityscape. Unfortunately, the good feeling ended at the front door. The presence of a sterile closed-circuit television screen (to see guests coming and going) and a chilly reception could not compensate for the lovely surroundings. Attitude makes all the difference.

It is important to remember that nothing remains the same. Ownership changes, prices go up, establishments shut down. I have tried to select those establishments that stand out in some (sometimes subtle) ways. You will find descriptions of B&Bs, guesthouses, country inns, small hotels, and farms. With one exception (Nairn's in Glasgow), breakfast is included, which is as it should be. (Nairn's is such an exceptional place that I have chosen to include it anyway.) Write us at the publisher's address with your comments—good or bad. We would love to hear from you about the listings and any new ones that you could recommend for the next edition.

GUARANTEE OF STANDARDS

The Scottish Tourist Board is the official guarantor of quality when it comes to accommodations in Scotland. The new Scottish Tourist Board star system is reportedly the first such system in the world to show the quality level of accommodation by using a star system. The more stars the better the quality. Hence, five stars refers to exceptional or world-class quality, four stars to excellent, three stars to very good, two stars to good, and one star to fair and acceptable.

A trained Scottish Tourist Board inspector grades each property annually. Further information on the star system can be obtained from the British Tourist Authority or at the various tourist information centers throughout Scotland.

A B&B in a private house generally starts from around £15 per person, although it can be considerably higher in the cities, especially in places like Edinburgh, depending on the location. Generally speaking, I have chosen to quote either single or double rates (some establishments do not offer single rates at all), based on per-person per-night charges. A B&B usually includes a full Scottish breakfast, and often a snack (biscuits, shortbread, and such) in the evening. (Either way, most rooms have tea- and/or coffee-making facilities). Many B&Bs, especially those in more remote areas, also offer dinner, although at an extra cost. Quite often the dinners at B&Bs are of a higher caliber than those found in local restaurants.

Most hosts will charge an additional few pounds for private facilities. Given today's competitive climate, where more and more travelers expect higher standards no matter how small the establishment, many B&B owners try to provide *ensuite* accommodations; that is, a room that contains a private bath and/or shower with toilet and sink. Sometimes the host offers a private bath, which can refer to a bath and/or shower that may be located down the hallway or outside your door, but one that is to be used exclusively by you or your traveling companion.

If you are coming to Scotland at the height of the high season—generally June, July, and August—it is best to book in advance. At any time, though, it is highly recommended that you book the first night of your stay no matter what time of the year. You can book before you arrive in several ways: 1) by contacting the individual establishments yourself; 2) through a travel agent; 3) through a major hotel's reservation service; or 4) through the Scottish Tourist Board's Internet site.

When in Scotland you can also book through the tourist information center's local booking service for a minimal fee of around £1, or by using the national Book-A-Bed Ahead service at the various tourist information centers around the country. This service enables you to arrange accommodations for the same evening or several nights in advance in another part of the country. It costs £3 and you must also pay a 10 percent returnable deposit.

All B&Bs listed have either been visited by myself or come highly recommended by friends or professional contacts within the Scottish tourist industry. The B&Bs in the *Scottish Bed & Breakfast Book* are held to our highest standards. Please contact us with your compliments or suggestions, or if you find that any of the lodgings fail to meet your expectations.

PRACTICAL MATTERS

Getting There

There are direct flights to Scotland from several North American destinations, including New York, Chicago (seasonal only), Newark, and Toronto. There are also flights from many European cities, including Amsterdam, Bergen, Brussels, Copenhagen, Dublin, Paris, Reykjavik, and Stavanger. For current information, check with your travel agent or consult the Scottish Tourist Board's latest flight information from your country at www.holiday.scotland.net/os.

In addition, many flight connections can be made within Scotland and to Scotland from other regional airports throughout the United Kingdom.

Money and Changing Currency

By all means do bring traveler's checks. You will feel more comfortable and self-assured for doing so. I would also strongly recommend for both your own benefit and the convenience of the other business party that they be in pounds sterling.

Banks are usually open Monday to Friday, between 9 A.M. to 4 or 5 P.M. Some banks are open late on Thursdays and a few are even open on Saturday mornings. Scottish banks issue their own bank notes that are legal tender in England as well (no matter what the English say). Banks usually offer the best exchange rates. Of course it is also possible to change money in airports, some of the larger railway stations, with travel agents, and the larger hotels (but only if you are a resident). There is usually a small handling fee and commission involved.

Credit cards are widely accepted throughout Scotland, although smaller accommodations or accommodations in more remote areas may not accept them. I have found that VISA is more accepted than MasterCard or American Express. Even so, it is always advisable to carry at least some cash or pound sterling traveler's checks around with you.

TRANSPORTATION

Rental Cars

It is usually cheaper to rent your car before arriving in Scotland. Check with your local travel agent.

Major international rental car companies are all represented in Scotland; again it is best to book through your travel agent. Most companies require the driver to be between 23 and 70, while holding a current driving license for at least one year. Note: If you prefer an automatic transmission, it is imperative that you reserve in advance.

A word of advice about driving in Scotland's four major cities (Glasgow, Edinburgh, Aberdeen, and Dundee): Don't.

Another word of advice on driving in Scotland: Stay left. Scotland, like the rest of the United Kingdom, drives on the left side of the road. It's an easy thing to forget, especially in the heat of the moment or when you're ogling a particularly beautiful sight. Just to be on the safe side a friend of mine always plants a large handwritten "KEEP LEFT" sign on the dashboard of the driver's side. It serves as an unobtrusive mental reminder.

Any holder of an overseas driving license may for a period of up to one year drive a car in Britain. The speed on dual carriageways (two-lane roads) is 70 mph, on single carriageways 60 mph, and residential areas 30 mph, unless otherwise signposted. Throughout Britain, it is compulsory for all car occupants to wear seat belts, unless the rear seats are not so equipped.

Motorist's tip: Watch out for the white-on-brown with a blue thistle road signs showing National Tourist Routes and visitor attractions. There are 12 of these routes, which take you along quieter roads and through the countryside. They usually traverse some of the country's most spectacular scenery.

Buses

Scotland has an extensive bus network. Indeed, buses travel to the smallest of towns. Scottish Citylink, in particular, serves all major cities and towns in Scotland, as well as some of the more outlying locations. National Express operates several times daily from London to Edinburgh and Glasgow.

Numerous companies operate bus services to or in Scotland, such as Skye-ways Express or Highland Country Buses. Advanced reservations are not usually required. The following are some useful numbers:

To and within Scotland
Scottish Citylink Coaches
990-505050

National Express
990-808080

Remote communities often use the more than 140 local services of the Royal Mail Postbuses, which not only deliver mail but also transport passengers, when there is no other form of public transport, for a nominal fee. For schedules contact Tel.: 0131-228-7407.

Trains

Although train travel in Scotland (and throughout the rest of Britain, for that matter) is not what it used to be, with so much privatization going on, it is still infinitely better than the service on this side of the ocean. The wise and economically frugal traveler will take full advantage of it.

Scotland's rail service provides excellent InterCity services between all major U.K. cities, as well as good internal links. The journey from London to Edinburgh, for example, takes about four hours, and about five hours from London to Glasgow. GNER, Virgin, and ScotRail operate rail services to points within Scotland. ScotRail publishes a monthly complimentary magazine, *Horizons,* which is available on most of the major lines.

For more information contact ScotRail by telephone at 0191-269-0203, consult their web site at www.scotrail.co.uk, or contact British Rail international branches:

Canada
Rail Europe
2087 Dundas Street East, #105
Mississauga, Ontario L4X 1M2

United States
BritRail
1500 Broadway, 10th floor
New York, NY 10036
Telephone: 212-382-3737
Fax: 212-575-2542

Ferries

Scotland has almost 800 islands, of which some 130 are inhabited. Caledonian MacBrayne (Tel.: 990-650000) offers services to 23 islands and 54 ports off the west coast and in the Firth of Clyde; most carry vehicles and passengers. The summer schedule operates from Easter to mid-October, although there is reduced service the rest of the year.

Other ferry services include Western Ferries (0141-332-9766), P&O Scottish Ferries (1224-572615), John o'Groats Ferries (1955-611353), Orkney Ferries (1856-872044), and Shetland Islands Council ferries (1806-244234).

Weather

People don't usually come to Scotland for the weather. They come in spite of it. That's just a way of saying that Scottish weather is unpredictable.

May and June are usually the driest months. The east coast tends to be cool and dry, the west milder and wetter. But these are only general guidelines, and within minutes upon your arrival in Scotland may be proven resolutely wrong. The average daily temperature during the summer months is 15-22 degrees centigrade.

Best piece of advice: layer. No matter how warm it may be during the day, always have another layer of clothing handy. You never know when the weather is going to change. Although it may be a bit bulky, you'll appreciate the extra warmth and comfort of the layers when the wind changes direction and the temperatures dip precipitously. And during those lucky instances when you are absolutely roasting, simply shed, shed, and shed again (within reason, of course).

BOOKING AHEAD

Booking Outside Scotland

It is always wise to book ahead, especially during high season. And even if departing during the shoulder season (May or September), it's still a good idea to book at least for the first night. That way you'll feel more secure knowing that when you land the next morning—all bleary-eyed and ready for a real bed—you'll at least know you have a place to rest your weary body.

If calling from the United States dial 1, then 011 (the international code), then 44 (the country code), and then the phone number itself. Typically no advance payment or credit card is required to hold a room.

Booking Inside Scotland

Booking ahead in Scotland is even easier. You simply phone the host and tell them approximately what time you will be arriving. In addition, many hosts would be more than happy to book ahead for you at no extra charge if you ask.

GENERAL INFORMATION ABOUT LODGINGS

Rooms

Generally speaking, the bedrooms in Scotland are smaller than what most North Americans are probably accustomed to. I have tried to choose accommodations that have character or are in some way unique. Ambiance goes far in this book.

Meals

Upon arrival, many hosts will offer you tea. Now mind you, "tea" is not merely a cup of the ubiquitous liquid, but rather a full repast all its own: it could include scones, tea breads, biscuits, shortbread, or other homemade goodies. (In Scotland you don't need to go to bed on an empty stomach if you don't want to.) When you arrive, do remind the host of any special or vegetarian dietary requests. If you arrive earlier in the day, you may discuss dinner plans with your host.

A full Scottish breakfast typically consists of eggs cooked to order, bacon, sausage, tomatoes (usually the stewed variety), toast or bread with butter or jam, juice, and cereal (muesli is on most menus; porridge is less common nowadays). Yogurt and fresh fruit or fruit compotes are increasingly showing up on breakfast menus. And don't be too surprised to find salmon, kippers, and occasionally haggis on your breakfast plate too.

Booking Tours and Events

Your host will be more than happy to book any tours or shows in the area. I have found that most B&B owners try to keep up with what's happening in their immediate vicinity. At the very least, they usually have brochures describing upcoming attractions.

Telephoning in Scotland

Inside Scotland you can phone with coins or with a phone card. Phone cards can be bought at post offices, news agents, and tourist information centers. Since hotels charge such high rates, you're better off using public telephones. Some of the B&Bs have coin box telephones where you can make local calls for 20 pence or so (keep your coins handy just in case).

When phoning from outside Scotland, dial your country's international access code (11 in the United States; xx in Canada) followed by 44. Then dial the area code minus the first 0 and then the phone number.

Scotland on the Web

For those who prefer to obtain their information quickly and with little effort, there are several Web sites that may be of use:

British Tourist Authority Web site:
www.visitbritain.com
www.holiday.scotland.net/os

Edinburgh and Scotland Information Centre Web site:
www.edinburgh.org

Glasgow Tourist Information Centre e-mail:
TourismGlasgow@ggcvtb.org.uk

Laundry

Because of their size, most B&Bs do not have laundry service—at least officially. Having said that, there have been numerous times when a B&B owner, perhaps taking pity on my limited wardrobe supply, offered to do my laundry free of charge. Although not a common occurrence, it can—and does—happen.

Handicapped Facilities

Although it still leaves a lot to be desired, Scotland offers a wide range of facilities suitable for people with disabilities. These include visitor attractions, accommodations, and shops. The Scottish Tourist Board produces an information guide designed to assist visitors with disabilities to find appropriate sources. For further information contact:

Disability Scotland
Princes House
5 Shandwick Place
Edinburgh EH2 4RG
Telephone: 0131-229-8632
Fax: 0131-229-5168

Security

Scotland is generally a safe country. But, as with most countries today, crime is on the upswing, especially in urban areas. It's best to lock your car at all times, and by all means keep your valuables in the trunk or simply out of plain sight. Although as a woman traveling alone I have never experienced any trouble, it is best to always keep your wits about you, especially at night or in unfamiliar areas.

The **Scottish Bed & Breakfast**
Book

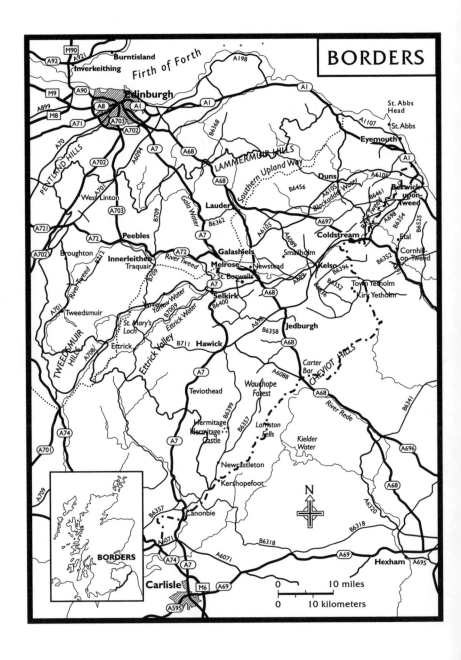

Borders

The Borders is best described as the land that got away. It is one of the more subtly beautiful parts of Scotland, and also an area that exudes an aura of tranquility, which is ironic given the area's violent past.

The name that is intricately associated with the Borders is Sir Walter Scott. Abbotsford House, his expansive estate and now a fine museum, is located just three miles west of the town of Melrose. Any visit to Abbotsford will showcase his study, library (with its more than 9,000 volumes shelved away), drawing room, armoires, and dining room overlooking the Tweed. It was here that he died in September 1832.

The Borders covers an area of approximately 1,800 square miles. It is a surprisingly diverse landscape that ranges from gently rolling hills to rocky coasts. The Borders also contains one of the longest rivers in Britain, the Tweed, which runs for about 100 miles through the area and at one point forms the natural border between Scotland and England.

For more than 300 years, from the late fourteenth century to the Union of Crowns in 1603, the Borders witnessed an endless succession of feuds and thievery, violence and turmoil. Blood flowed all too often through its streams and rivers. Perhaps it is because of this deep-rooted anguish that the Borders offers one of the richest folk cultures in the country. The ordinary men and women of the area created their own musical genre—that of the Border ballads, wild and wildly entertaining stories populated by a larger-than-life cast of characters and fraught with the very real prospect of danger.

More than most areas of Scotland, Border towns seem especially keen on promoting a very high level of community involvement. This is most visibly expressed in the fervor associated with the local sport, rugby, but also in the Common Ridings that take place throughout the summer months, when everybody seems to get involved. These annual events commemorate a time when community boundaries required protection from outsiders.

Elsewhere in the Borders you will find excellent woolen mills and shops, as well as the romance of the great, and ruined, Border abbeys, particularly Melrose, Jedburgh, Kelso, and Dryburgh. Scott is buried here amid the abbey ruins. What a suitably romantic site indeed for this most romantic of Scottish figures! The Border towns of Selkirk, Peebles, and Hawick are also worth visiting.

One of the moodiest of castles is Hermitage Castle, which sits in splendid isolation along a remote tract of road in a lonely glen. It's not easy to get to, but what a sight to behold when you eventually arrive: a marvelous relic of a castle, squat and foreboding and full of deep, dark secrets. Mary Queen of Scots spent several hours here in 1566, and they're still talking about it.

Burts Hotel
Graham, Ann, and Nicholas Henderson
Market Square
Melrose
Telephone: 01896-822285
Fax: 01896-822870
E-mail: burtshotel@aol.com
Web site: www.melrose.bordernet.com.uk.
Bedrooms: 20, all ensuite.
Rates: £44-50 pp. **Credit cards:** MasterCard/Eurocard, American
Express, VISA, Diners Club, Switch, Delta, JCB. **Open:** All year except
December 24-27. **Children:** Yes. **Pets:** Dogs only. **Smoking:** No smoking
in bedrooms and restaurant; smoking in bar and bistro only. **Provision
for handicapped:** Yes. **Directions:** On the A6091, 2 miles from A68,
38 miles south of Edinburgh. Located in the town square.

This restored family-run eighteenth-century hotel is ably and cheerfully run by the Henderson family: Graham, Anne, and Nicholas. Set
in the town's market square, Burts has been a local landmark for generations—it was built in 1722 as a comfortable home for a prominent
local. Although the historic building has been thoroughly modernized, it still retains its period charm. For more than 25 years it has
been personally overseen by Graham and Anne. Over the years they
have been joined in the family business by their son Nicholas and his
wife Trish. Each room is individually decorated. Sitting for a few
moments by the glowing fireplace or having a drink in the lounge
bar is a pleasant way to start the evening. The bar has over 60 malt
whiskies. You are also welcome to enjoy the private hotel garden.

There's a comfortable resident's lounge on the first floor, and a Taste of Scotland restaurant on the premises that specializes in local game, fish, and poultry, seasonal salads, veggies, and fruits. Fare specific to the Borders might include wedges of Teviotdale cheese with smoked salmon, served with a whiskey marmalade, followed by a Border lamb rolled with wild mushrooms and spinach and accompanied by minted apple chutney. For dessert, try the Selkirk bannock pudding with lemon and shortbread ice cream. The Borders has 19 golf courses. Melrose's golf club is located in an elevated position, with views over Scott country.

Dunfermline House Guest House
Susan and Ian Graham
Buccleuch Street
Melrose
Telephone/Fax: 01896-822148
E-mail: bestaccom@dunmel.freeserve.co.uk
Web site: www.melrose.bordernet.co.uk
Bedrooms: 5; 4 ensuite, 1 single with private bathroom.
Rates: £25. **Credit cards:** No. **Open:** Yes. **Children:** Yes. **Pets:** No.
Smoking: No. **Provision for handicapped:** No. **Directions:** From
Melrose follow directions for Melrose Abbey. Dunfermline House is
opposite the Abbey car park.

The Grahams own a handsome Victorian townhouse that is located
in a former town saddlery. It is now one of the longest established
and most respected guesthouses in the area and, best of all, conveniently located about 50 yards from famous Melrose Abbey. The
abbey, a warm reddish sandstone ruin, has a terrific history of its own
to tell. Founded in 1136 by Cistercian monks at the behest of King
David I, Melrose soon became one of the wealthiest monasteries in
Scotland and held one of the largest sheep farms in Europe. Time and
raiding took its toll over the centuries. What you see today is mostly
from the fifteenth and sixteenth centuries. After poking around the
romantic ruins or sightseeing around the surrounding countryside,
the Grahams offer a cozy place to return to. Don't forget to try their
traditionally made porridge and homemade jams and marmalades in
their comfortable dining room.

Tibbie Shiels Inn
Mrs. J. Brown
St. Mary's Loch
Selkirkshire
Telephone: 01750-42231
Bedrooms: 5 rooms; 1 with bath, 4 with showers.
Rates: £24 single. **Credit cards:** VISA, Delta, MasterCard. **Open:** Closed Monday, Tuesday, and Wednesday from November to Easter.
Children: Yes. **Pets:** No. **Smoking:** Yes. **Provision for handicapped:** Yes.
Directions: Situated between St. Mary's Loch and the Loch of the Lowes on the A708 Selkirk to Moffat Road.

Tibbie Shiels must surely be one of the most famous historical inns in Scotland. Established in 1826, this whitewashed lodging has strong associations with Sir Walter Scott, William Wordsworth, and James Hogg. Indeed, a statue of a seated Mr. Hogg stands across the busy road. Situated on the isthmus between St. Mary's Loch and the Loch of the Lowes, it takes its name from Isabella (Tibbie) Shiel, who moved with her husband Robert Richardson, a mole catcher, in 1823 into what was then known as St. Mary's Cottage, on the estate of Lord Napier. After the death of her husband the following year, the irrepressible Tibbie determined to support herself and her six children by taking in "gentlemen lodgers." Tibbie apparently had a great sense of humor, and there are countless stories that attest to that. She died in 1878 in her 96th year, but until then she forever played the charming hostess. Publisher Robert Chambers was an early visitor, while another regular was the aforementioned Mr. Hogg, the writer and poet (best known today for his psychological novel *The Private Memoirs and Confessions of a Justified Sinner).* It seems that Tibbie was an old friend of Hogg—she had worked as a girl in his mother's household—and was totally unimpressed by his writing. Other prominent visitors included Robert Louis Stevenson, Thomas Carlyle, and Prime Minister William Gladstone. It's still a popular stop, especially for those walking the Southern Upland Way. Sailing and windsurfing are available on the loch. As to be expected in such a venerable place, the low-ceilinged inn is cozy and full of great character. Afternoon tea is available from £3.75, high tea from £8, and dinner from £5-11.50. Free fishing is available for guests.

Gordon Arms Hotel
John McCann
Yarrow
By Selkirk
Telephone: 01750-82232
Bedrooms: 6 rooms.
Rates: £26 pp. **Credit cards:** No. **Open:** Year-round. **Children:** Yes.
Pets: Yes. **Smoking:** Yes. **Provision for handicapped:** No.**Directions:**
Between Selkirk and Moffat on the A708 Road.

This family-run and historic hotel lies along the A708 just west of
Selkirk. Literary fans should especially find it significant, for here
reportedly took place the last meeting between Sir Walter Scott and
James Hogg. Scott is of course the great Scots novelist and Hogg an
important writer and poet in his own right. From a Borders perspective, what makes it even more fascinating is that both figures were
prominent ballad collectors as well. And the area around the Gordon
Arms has rich associations with the great Border ballad tradition.
Indeed, one of the most poignant and heartbreakingly sad of the ballads, "The Dowie Dens o' Yarrow," is set in this area. The current
owner, John McCann, is an ex-firefighter, so one suspects that he has
quite a few tales of his own to share with his guests. Good home cooking is offered at the Gordon Arms, while homemade bread is a specialty. Real ales and single malt whiskies are on tap. Hillwalking,
cycling, and fishing are just some of the outdoor activities available in
the immediate area.

ALSO RECOMMENDED

Duns, *St. Albans,* Mrs. Hannay, Clouds Lane. Telephone: 01361-883285. Fax: 01361-884534. 1 room, with private facilities. Attractive Georgian house with tranquil and secluded garden. Offers magnificent views over the Cheviot Hills. Quiet location. Non-smoking.

By **Eyemouth,** *Redhall Cottages,* Joan Binns, Ayton. Telephone: 018907-81488. 3 rooms, all ensuite. Utterly charming cottages in a very quiet setting. Golf packages are available. No children. Non-smoking.

Innerleithen, *Caddon View Guest House,* 14 Pirn Road. Telephone: 01896-830208. 6 rooms; 5 ensuite and 1 private. Victorian-era home known for its French home cooking. Free use of sauna.

Innerleithen, *St. Ronans Hotel,* Peeblesshire. Telephone: 01896-831487. 6 rooms. Family-owned and operated 1820s historic inn. Past guests have included none other than Sir Walter Scott and Robert Burns. Handsome textured white brick exterior.

Kelso, *Bellevue House,* Bowmont Street. Telephone/Fax: 01573-224588. 6 rooms, all ensuite. Charming building built in the 1860s and once home to the angler and poet Thomas Stoddart. Non-smoking. Near town center, Floors Castle, and the River Tweed.

Melrose, *Bon Accord Hotel,* Market Square. Telephone: 01896-822645. Fax: 01896-823474. 10 rooms, all ensuite. Small cheery hotel with modern conveniences. Located in the heart of town.

Melrose, *Little Fordel,* Louise Buchanan, Abbey Street. Telephone: 01896-822206. 2 rooms, both ensuite. Pretty B&B housed in a former schoolhouse and located in a quiet cul-de-sac in the center of town.

Peebles, *The Horse Shoe Inn,* Mr. and Mrs. Hathaway, Eddleston. Telephone: 01721-730225. Fax: 01721-730268. E-mail: Derek.hathaway@virgin.net. Web site: www.horseshoeinn.com. 8 rooms. Small, charming country inn on the outskirts of Peebles.

Peebles, *Lindores,* Mr. and Mrs. C. Lane, Old Town. Telephone/Fax: 01721-720441. E-mail: lane.lindores@virgin.net. 4 rooms, 2 ensuite. Excellent food is served by an award-winning chef in this spacious and attractive house.

By **Peebles,** *The Shieling,* John and Joan Richardson, Eshiels. Telephone/Fax: 01721-722577. 3 rooms, 1 ensuite. Modern country house located in half-acre garden. Offers lovely views over the Tweed Valley. Located about .5 mile from Peebles.

St. Boswells, *The Clachan,* Nina Johnstone, Main Street. Telephone: 01835-822266. 3 rooms. Large, comfy home located on the edge of the village of St. Boswells. Boasts a log fire. Close to the River Tweed, fishing, and golf. Evening meals served. Walkers please note: this is a perfect location for walking St. Cuthbert's Way, a 2.5-mile pilgrimage route that stretches from Melrose to Lindisfarne in England.

St. Boswells, *Greenside Farm,* Moira Steel, by Melrose. Telephone: 01835-822140. 6 rooms, all ensuite. Victorian farmhouse located in the center of the small village of St. Boswells.

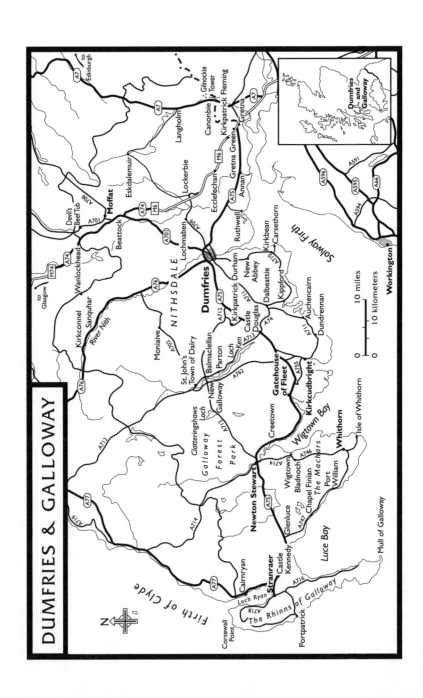

DUMFRIES & GALLOWAY

Dumfries & Galloway

Dumfries and Galloway has everything that many visitors to Scotland would desire—sparkling lochs, moody peaks, rolling hills, smart and attractive towns, and enough outdoor activities to keep even the most active traveler busy for days on end.

Yet this area remains one of Scotland's most neglected corners. Perhaps the reason for the neglect is its location, a relatively remote section in the southwestern corner of the country, or perhaps it has more to do with its low profile. Whatever the reason, it is a shame, for Dumfries and Galloway has a lot to offer.

The commercial center of the region is Dumfries, an attractive big town that has rich associations with Robert Burns, Scotland's national bard (the Burns Statue is located smack in the center of town). Burns spent his last years here. He and his family lived at the house on Burns Street, now called the Burns House, until his death in 1796. Burns also spent many an enjoyable hour at the famous Globe Inn, off High Street. This is truly a wonderful place—with or without Burns. It boasts great atmosphere, friendly service, and terrific food. An inn since 1610, it contains much of interest to Burns enthusiasts and non-enthusiasts alike: his favorite chair, bowl, and ladle, and if you ask a staff member they will take you upstairs to see where the poet etched a few stanzas in the bedroom window.

Dumfries and Galloway contains several pretty small towns and villages. During the eighteenth and early nineteenth centuries, Gatehouse of Fleet was a solid cotton manufacturing town. James Murray, the local laird, planned the building of the town and the erection of the mills. The Bobbin Mill, the last remnant in Gatehouse of the Industrial Revolution, closed as recently as the 1930s and has since been converted into an award-winning museum. It is certainly worth a visit.

However, no town in the district is as charming as Kirkcudbright, strategically and handsomely located on a harbor. Take the time to leisurely walk down its narrow streets. Palm trees, attractive old houses, and a mild climate drew many artists here, as early as the 1880s. But its art colony credentials really came to complete fruition in the late 1920s, when artists such as E.A. Hornel, Jessie M. King, and S.J. Peploe, among others, either settled or summered here. The work of contemporary artists is on display at places like the Harbour Cottage Gallery and the Tolbooth Arts Centre.

Historic figures also left their mark in Dumfries and Galloway. Thomas Carlyle, the crusty man of letters who later moved to London and became known as the "Sage of Chelsea," was born in the town of Ecclefechan. His house is located here, off the A74, where you can view his collection of photographs, manuscripts, letters, and other related paraphernalia.

It's hard to believe that the origins of the American navy lie in this part of the world. Yet it was here in Kirkbean, in a corner of Scotland known as the Garden of Galloway, that John Paul Jones was born in a small, whitewashed, two-room cottage. There is a museum and audio-visual program that relates the young naval hero's victories during the Revolutionary War. It also includes a recreation of the cabin aboard his ship, the *Bonhomme Richard.*

Moffat boasts having the widest main street in Scotland. This former sheep and wool trading center is best symbolized by the bronze statue of the Moffat Ram that stands proudly on High Street. Woolen shops as well as ice cream and toffee shops line the broad thoroughfare.

Much of what you see today dates from the nineteenth century, when Moffat was known as a Victorian spa town and flocks of people came here, by railway in those days, to savor its soothing mineral waters. The local Moffat Museum, housed in a former bakery, tells the story of Moffat, including its days as a popular spa center.

Moffat is fortunate to be near several natural landmarks that are worth seeking out. The Grey Mare's Tail on the A708 refers to a spectacular 200-foot waterfall, while the Devil's Beeftub on the A701 is a natural depression used by reivers, or thieves, for hiding stolen cattle in the bad old days.

Another town worth visiting is Whithorn, a market center that is surrounded by many fascinating archeological sites and monuments. Most fascinating of all is the cult of St. Ninian, Scotland's first saint, which flourished in the area for more than a thousand years. Ninian is said to have built his small stone church, the Candida Casa, or White House, here, said to be the first Christian church in Scotland. The Whithorn Priory and Museum along the main street contains the ruins of a twelfth-century priory. Whithorn was also a popular place of pilgrimage, especially for Scottish monarchs. While here, do take the time to visit the Whithorn Discovery Centre, which tells the story of Scotland's first Christian settlement—archeologists have been excavating the site since 1986. Their discoveries are also on display at the center.

The town of Newton Stewart is a good base for forays into Galloway Forest Park, which is studded with lochs, woods, and hills. If you really want to go off the beaten track, though, then hightail it to the Rhinns of Galloway, the peninsula that juts out into the Irish Sea. The southern portion of the peninsula will eventually take you to the Mull of Galloway, with its splendid views of Ireland, the Isle of Man, Cumbria in England, and the Galloway Hills.

The Auldgirth Inn
Peter and Sarah Landale
Auldgirth
Telephone/Fax: 01387-740250
Bedrooms: 3 rooms, 2 ensuite.
Rates: £40 double. **Credit cards:** VISA, Switch, MasterCard, Solo, JCB.
Open: All year. **Children:** Yes. **Pets:** Yes. **Smoking:** In public areas only.
Provision for handicapped: Yes. **Directions:** From Dumfries take the A76 to Auldgirth, some 8 miles out of town. The inn is located just off the A76, on the road north of Dumfries.

This inn dates back to the 1500s, when it was used by monks and pilgrims as a stopover from Melrose Abbey to the Galloway abbeys. "Auldgirth" is Scots for "old sanctuary." Remnants of its earlier spiritual connections are represented by a cross on the large, central chimney. Later, Robert Burns, Scotland's national bard, used it as his local watering hole when it functioned as both an inn and a smithy. Today the modernized inn has simply decorated rooms. Nothing fancy perhaps, but they are warm and comfortable, which is a reassuring thought when on the road. There are two bars downstairs: the Fisherman's Bar has an open fire and serves meals at lunchtime and in the evening; the Bothy Restaurant has its own bar and is bright and cheery. The Landales pride themselves on serving the best of local produce. The beef and lamb, for example, are from a neighboring estate, and the free-range eggs are from the farm next door. Fish comes from the River Nith, which conveniently runs practically past their door. "We pretend to be no more than a comfortable, cozy, country inn, with our main emphasis on really good food and a very personal service," they say. And it shows.

Murray Arms Hotel
Ann Street
Gatehouse-of-Fleet
Telephone: 01557-814207
Fax: 01557-814370
Bedrooms: 13 rooms, all ensuite.
Rates: £49.50 pp. **Credit cards:** American Express, MasterCard, Diners Club, VISA. **Open:** All year. **Pets:** Yes. **Smoking:** Restricted. **Provision for handicapped:** No. **Directions:** Off the A75, midway between Dumfries and Stranraer. The hotel is located by the clock tower.

Established over 300 years ago, this old coach inn was also patronized by Robert Burns. Indeed, the peripatetic poet wrote "Scots Wha Hae," one of his most famous songs and Scotland's unofficial national anthem, here. Ask to see the Burns Room, where he actually wrote the poem. The hotel has 13 comfortable rooms, 3 public rooms (bars), and the Lunky Hole Restaurant, which makes good use of Galloway's fine produce. The town's name derives from the Gate House, a protective wall that dates from circa 1760. In addition to Burns, generations of Scots and visitors alike have spent many a pleasant night at the Murray Arms. Except for a brief time, for most of its history the Murray Arms has been part of the Cally Estate. James Murray of Broughton and Cally built the inn in 1760. The portion of the building that is now used as the coffee room existed prior to 1642, and was at one time the only house in town (referred to as the Gait House). The keeper of the gait, or road to the ford across the River Fleet, lived here. Within walking distance from the inn are many historical buildings, including the Mill on the Fleet, which served as the center of the town's once-flourishing cotton industry.

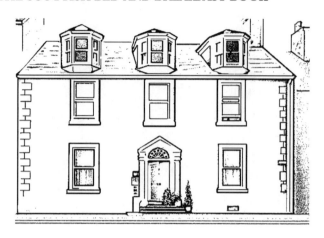

Baytree House
Jackie Callander and Robert Watson
110 High Street
Kirkcudbright
Telephone/Fax: 01557-330824
E-mail: baytree@currantbun.com
Bedrooms: 4 rooms, all ensuite.
Rates: £27-30. **Credit cards:** None. **Open:** All year. **Children:** All ages. **Pets:** Small pets. **Smoking:** No. **Provision for handicapped:** Two ground floor bedrooms are large enough for wheelchairs. **Directions:** Travel along the main A75 route going west. Take the 711 road to Kirkcudbright. Drive straight through town until you come to High Street. Baytree is located halfway along the road, at the junction of High and Castle Streets.

Located near the harbor in the old quarter of this pretty artist's colony, Baytree is an old Georgian townhouse with the original wood-work and fireplaces still intact. Its impressive drawing room comes complete with vaulted ceiling and ornate cornices. There is also a huge drawing room on the first floor, with an open fire. Jackie and Robert moved to the area in 1995, thoroughly renovated the house, and opened for business in February 1997. The enterprising couple also created their own garden (about .75 acres altogether), consid-ered one of the finest in Kirkcudbright, which contains a small pond surrounded by old stone walls. One of the Baytree's double rooms has a fourposter bed and Victorian bath. The garden room is a self-contained unit, with its own kitchen, bathroom, bed, and even its own conservatory (glass-covered area), where you can have breakfast served. Hence, those who stay in the garden room can come and go as they please. Each room retains its own personality though, and is tastefully decorated. In warm weather, you can sit and relax on the sundeck. The B&B also contains a fine collection of antiques and paintings, the latter by Kirkcudbright artists. All the food is homemade. A typical breakfast may consist of scrambled eggs made with cream and served with smoked salmon and fennel. A traditional clootie dumpling (a pudding typically made with butter, syrup, treacle, egg, milk, and flour) comes accompanied with a traditional Scottish breakfast. Dinner is a treat, too. Jackie and Robert use all local game and fish (salmon, scallops, trout, etc.) as well as fresh raspberries and strawberries from the garden. Afternoon teas are also offered. Kirkcudbright is known for its mild climate. It even boasts palm trees.

Selkirk Arms Hotel
John and Susan Morris
High Street
Kirkcudbright
Telephone: 01557-330402
Fax: 01557-331639
Bedrooms: 17 rooms, all ensuite.
Rates: £65 pp. **Credit cards:** MasterCard/Eurocard, American Express, VISA, Diners Club, Switch, Delta, JCB. **Open:** All year except Christmas Day. **Children:** Yes. **Pets:** Yes. **Provision for handicapped**: Restricted.
Directions: Located on the east end of Kirkcudbright's High Street.

The Selkirk Arms, located on a quiet residential street, is probably the best-known hotel in Kirkcudbright, and certainly one of the oldest. Dating back to 1770, this historic hotel has witnessed many changes in the area and played host to many visitors (Robert Burns stayed here in 1794, and it was here that he wrote "The Selkirk Grace"). Today's owners, John and Susan Morris, continue in that grand tradition. The modernized version of the Selkirk Arms serves several functions. On the one hand it is most certainly a handsome hostelry, providing all the amenities that the contemporary traveler expects and, indeed, demands. But it also houses a fine gourmet restaurant, where the service is professional and the staff friendly without being overbearing. The restaurant overlooks a large and secluded garden. The coat of arms on the hotel sign belongs to Thomas Douglas, the Earl of Selkirk, a Kirkcudbright native and the man responsible for the founding of what would become the modern Canadian city of Winnipeg. A short walk away from the hotel, the Broughton House and Gardens is a handsome Georgian mansion and the former home of E. A. Hornel, considered the founder of Kirkcudbright's artist's colony. The museum contains many of Hornel's paintings and a Japanese-style garden in the back.

ALSO RECOMMENDED

Ecclefechan, *Cressfield Country House Hotel,* Mr. and Mrs. Arthur, Townfoot, Dumfries-shire. Telephone: 01576-300281. Fax: 01576-204218. 10 rooms, all ensuite. This handsome sandstone building was constructed in the nineteenth century and was designed by Thomas Carlyle's father.

Gatehouse-of-Fleet, *The Bay House,* Carole Jackson, 9 Ann Street. Telephone: 01557-814073. 3 rooms, 2 ensuite. A lovely B&B, small and cozy, overlooking garden, with a riot of flowers overflowing from windowsills. Peaceful setting any way you look at it.

Gatehouse-of-Fleet, *The Cree Gallery,* Linda Hepburn, 56 High Street. Telephone/Fax: 01557-814458. 2 rooms; 1 double and 1 family. Comfortable accommodation situated above an art gallery and antique shop. The work of contemporary artists from England and Scotland is on display. And in an unusual twist, breakfast is served in the gallery.

Kirkbean, *Cavens House Hotel,* Kirkbean, by Dumfries. Telephone/Fax: 01387-880234. 6 rooms, all ensuite. Fairly large estate built by Glasgow tobacco lord Robert Oswald, who reportedly had close connections with none other than Benjamin Franklin.

Kirkcudbright, *Gladstone House,* Susan and James Westbrook, 48 High Street. Telephone/Fax: 01557-331734. 3 rooms, all ensuite. Georgian townhouse near the harbor, castle, art galleries, and restaurants. Afternoon teas are served in the elegant drawing room or secluded garden. No smoking.

Kirkcudbright, *1 Gordon Place,* Heather Black, High Street. Telephone: 01557-330472. 2 rooms with private facilities. Immaculately clean 200-year-old house opposite Broughton House. Very lovely.

Kirkpatrick Fleming, *The Mill,* Kathleen M. Smith, Grahamshill. Telephone: 01461-800344 or 01461-800603. Fax: 01461-800255. 24 rooms, all ensuite. Converted farmstead built circa 1750. Located in a tranquil setting on the outskirts of Gretna Green.

Moffat, *Alba House,* Evelyn Lindsay, 20 Beechgrove. Telephone/Fax: 01683-220418. 2 rooms, both ensuite. Built circa 1730. Boasts a beamed dining room with inglenook. A few minutes' walk from town center.

Moffat, *Boleskine,* Sheila and Andy Armstrong, 4 Well Road. Telephone: 01683-220601. 4 rooms, 2 ensuite. The Armstrongs are a friendly couple who do their best to make you feel at home at their large Victorian house. Located on a quiet street a few minutes' walk from the town center. Good and healthy home cooking served.

Moffat, *Burnock Water,* David and Sheila Barclay, Haywood Road. Telephone: 01683-221329. 5 rooms, 3 ensuite. Comfortable Victorian family house with its own garden overlooking the Moffat hills. About .5 mile from town center.

Moniaive, *Park House,* Mrs. Bradley, Dunreggan. Telephone: 01848-200440. 2 rooms with private facilities. Artist-run family home located on the edge of historic Moniaive. Home baking their specialty.

New Abbey, *Criffel Inn,* 2 The Square, by Dumfries. Telephone: 01387-850305. 5 rooms, 4 ensuite. Family-run hotel in the pretty village of New Abbey. A short walk away from the evocatively romantic ruins of Sweetheart Abbey. Sandy beaches, golf, and sea angling opportunities also nearby.

By **Stranraer,** *Corsewall Lighthouse Hotel,* Jim Neilson, Kirkcolm. Telephone: 01776-853220. Fax: 01776-854231 E-mail: Jim-Neilson@msn.com. 6 rooms; 5 ensuite, 1 with private facilities. One of the more unusual hotels in Scotland. Situated on 20 acres in a former lighthouse, the hotel offers spectacular views and first-rate accommodations, with prices to match (from £50-100 double).

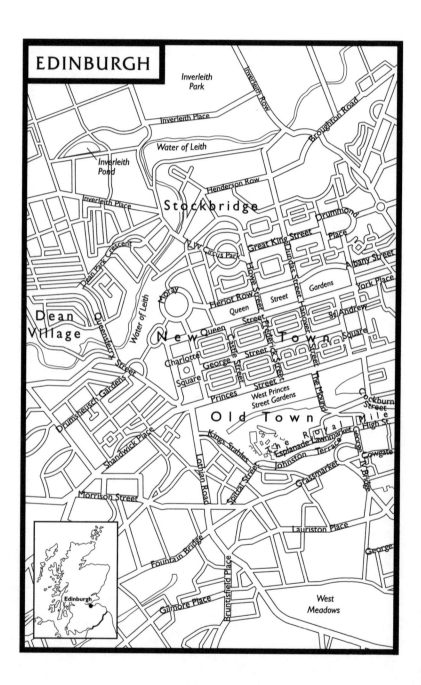

Edinburgh

In 1999 the Scottish Parliament returned to Edinburgh, a momentous occasion in the history of a country that has seen more than its share of triumphant as well as disastrous events. But the new Parliament seems to have rekindled a long-smoldering spirit of hope and optimism in this most famous of Scottish cities.

Part of this new spirit can best be exemplified in the fairly new—it opened in late 1998—Museum of Scotland, which contains the history of Scotland all under one roof, from its geological beginnings to the waning days of the twentieth century. The handsome structure, with its modified turret, acknowledges the past as it nods to the future.

Edinburgh is also a city of culture, from the almost embarrassing riches that comprise the Edinburgh International Festival each August to the daily diet of theater, nightlife, and fine restaurants that beckons both visitor and resident alike throughout the rest of the year.

Most visitors to this handsome city will undoubtedly spend most of their time in the Old Town and the New Town. In Edinburgh what constitutes "old" and "new" is relative. In this case the Old Town, or the Royal Mile, as it is also known, refers to the area, actually more than a mile in length, which stretches from brooding Edinburgh Castle to the Palace of Holyrood. This Royal Mile captures the spirit of another, darker era, of narrow passageways and dank tenements, of thievery and debauchery, and of lives lived in the shadow of crime and disease.

Fortunately, conditions have brightened considerably since then. Of course, the castle is a must. But other highlights include the Scotch Whisky Heritage Centre, where you'll learn more about Scotland's national drink than you ever thought possible; the Writer's Museum, a collection of memorabilia dedicated to that Caledonian trio of letters—Robert Burns, Sir Walter Scott, and Robert Louis Stevenson; the wonder of St. Giles Cathedral; as well as many other small museums, arts centers, coffeehouses, historic pubs, and old inns.

The New Town, on the other hand, was built in the eighteenth century. It's a genteel corner of the city consisting of elegant town-houses fronting parks, squares, and circles. Everything in the New Town exudes harmony, serenity, and reason, a sense of exquisite balance and an overall good feeling that all is right with the world.

Edinburgh's premier shopping street is Princes Street. Although probably not as significant as it once was, it is still a fine thoroughfare, lined with old-fashioned hotels and department stores, bookstores, and all kinds of shops, from tourist tacky to the subtly elegant. Across the street is the open expanse of the Princes Street Gardens. When the crowds become overwhelming it's reassuring to know that you're only a few steps away from a leafy haven.

Of the many cultural institutions that await you in Edinburgh, you should at least consider visiting the National Gallery of Scotland, the Scottish National Portrait Gallery, the Scottish National Gallery of Modern Art, and the Traverse Theatre, to name but a few.

Sibbet House
Jim Sibbet
26 Northumberland Street
Edinburgh
Telephone: 0131-556-1078
Fax: 0131-557-9445
E-mail: sibbet.house@zetnet.co.uk
Web site: www.sibbet-house.co.uk
Bedrooms: 4 plus one suite, all ensuite; 2 self-catering apartments also available.
Rates: £80-100 double. **Credit cards:** VISA, MasterCard, Switch, Access. **Smoking:** No. **Provision for handicapped:** Difficult. **Open:** Year-round. **Children:** No small children. **Pets:** Negotiable. **Directions:** Located in the heart of Edinburgh's New Town, a 10-minute walk from Princes Street.

This gorgeous New Town townhouse, built in 1809, is one of the real gems of Edinburgh, and you can't beat its wonderful location. With its antique furniture and oil paintings, Sibbet House truly represents fine living at its best and most elegant. As expected, the bedrooms are immaculate and luxuriously decorated. The walls are painted in deep warm colors, shimmering chandeliers hang from the ceiling, and a spiral staircase leads to opulent rooms full of canopied and four-poster beds. The upstairs formal drawing room reeks of wealth, recalling a more elegant time when status, station, and heredity determined your past, present, and future. From our modern vantage point, it's hard to believe that people actually lived in such opulence on a daily basis and thought nothing of it. Now you as an honored guest can get a glimpse into this long-departed world. The owner, Jim Sibbet (who was famous for playing a tune or two on his bagpipe whenever the urge came over him), has formally retired. Nowadays the day-to-day business affairs of running the establishment are conducted by a Danish couple, who also provide guided tours of the Edinburgh area and even venture as far away as Grampian and Fife.

27 Heriot Row
Andrea and Gene Targett-Adams
27 Heriot Row
Edinburgh
Telephone: 0131-220-1699
Fax: 0131-225-9474
E-mail: t.a@cableinet.co.uk
Bedrooms: 3 rooms, all ensuite.
Rates: £90 double. **Credit cards:** VISA, MasterCard. **Open:** Year-round.
Children: Yes. **Pets:** No. **Smoking:** No (although there is a "smoker's bench" outside). **Provision for handicapped:** No. **Directions:** Located in the New Town, directly across the street from Queen Street Gardens.

Imagine yourself in your very own private townhouse in the heart of Edinburgh's New Town, for that is the way that Gene and Andrea make you feel. These two urbane, witty, and sophisticated hosts make Heriot Row a cut above the rest. The rooms are impeccable, clean, stylish, and comfortable; the ambiance is utterly delightful, thanks in no small measure to the conversational skills of the owners; the service is above reproach. And then there are the breakfasts, including one of the few places in the country where I actually enjoyed French toast. Gene and Andrea are always ready to offer a word of advice to visitors. They try to keep up with new restaurant openings and other special events going on about town. Ask and you shall receive a thoughtful and considerate reply. Robert Louis Stevenson's childhood home at 17 Heriot Row is a few doors down. Another plus: you are given your own key with your own private entrance, so now your dream of having a place of your own in the New Town is all but assured—at least for a few nights or so.

41 Heriot Row
Erlend and Helene Clouston
41 Heriot Row
Edinburgh
Telephone: 0131-225-3113
Fax: 0131-225-3113
E-mail: erlendc@lineone.net
Bedrooms: 2 rooms, 1 with private shower.
Rates: £35 pp single, £50 double. **Credit cards:** Yes. **Open:** Year-round.
Children: Yes. **Pets:** No. **Smoking:** No. **Provision for handicapped:** No.
Directions: Located in the New Town, across from Queen Street
Gardens.

You've heard of The 39 Steps; well, the Clouston's sophisticated flat
could very well be given the nickname of "The 49 Steps," for that is the
number of gray stone steps that lead to their front door. Erlend and
Helene are a marvelous couple; he is a freelance journalist with roots
in Shetland, and she is a French schoolteacher. They live in their
expansive New Town quarters with a teenage son (another son is away
at school) and their two friendly cats Tom and Jerry. Friendly, charming, and warm, they are genuinely interested in learning more about
other cultures, as well as sharing their own cultures with guests. The
building itself was erected in 1817 as part of the northern extension of
the New Town. Red carpets lead to a skylight above the staircase. The
two rooms are spacious, with pine floors and brass beds. The views
from the bedrooms are simply stunning—the perfect place to watch
a peaceful sunrise, or sunset, over Edinburgh. The Cloustons offer
thoughtful touches, such as books by your bedside, mostly Scottish in

theme (Samuel Johnson and James Boswell's *Tour to the Hebrides*, *The Burns Encyclopedia*, Lewis Grassic Gibbon's *A Scots Quair.*) Breakfasts are healthy, tasty, and filling (ask for Erlend's Katmandu frozen yogurt; it's so good it should be patented so the rest of the world can enjoy it). The Cloustons have created a haven in the heart of the city.

40A Heriot Row
Diane and Robert Rae
40A Heriot Row
Edinburgh
Telephone: 0131-226-2068
Bedrooms: 2 rooms, ensuite.
Rates: £80 double. **Credit cards:** No. **Open:** Year-round. **Children:** Yes. **Pets:** No. **Smoking:** Restricted. **Provision for handicapped:** No. **Directions:** Located in the New Town, across from Queen Street Gardens.

The Raes run a lovely bed and breakfast in their smartly elegant New Town townhouse with great panache, style, and charm. Robert, a native of Edinburgh, is tall, bearded, and urbane, a perfect gentleman; Diane is from south of the Border, warm and conversational with no airs or pretenses about her. Each proves to be the perfect foil for the other, as well as being endlessly entertaining to their guests. The cozy and snug bedrooms are located in the lower level, safely ensconsced from the noise and hassle of the outside world. Breakfast is served in the book-lined dining room and can range from the simple (muesli, fresh fruit, toast, and tea or coffee) to the extravagant (a Sunday champagne brunch of smoked salmon and eggs, for example, or a plate of kippers and sometimes a slice of haggis). Guests have access to a hair dryer, shoe cleaning equipment, a clothes brush, complimentary body lotions and shampoos, and other little personal touches. The Raes make friends easily; once you have been here, you will want to return again and again.

ALSO RECOMMENDED

Edinburgh, *Balmoral Guest House,* Alex and Margaret MacKenzie, 32 Pilrig Street. Telephone: 0131-554-1857. 5 rooms. Small guesthouse, pleasant, clean, and comfortable, and close to the city center. The MacKenzies are a friendly couple and, with very little prodding, will eagerly dispense advice and travel tips to visitors to their favorite city.

Edinburgh, *Channings,* Peter and Mhairi Taylor, South Learmonth Gardens. Telephone: 0131-315-2226. Fax: 0131-332-9631. 48 rooms, all ensuite. A combination of five Edwardian townhouses on a quiet cobblestoned street in the New Town. Relaxed ambiance. Channings also houses the Brasserie, a fine restaurant of Scottish and French cooking.

Edinburgh, *Dene Guest House,* 7 Eyre Place. Telephone: 0131-556-2700. Fax: 0131-557-9876. Charming Georgian townhouse in a good location at affordable rates.

Edinburgh, *Drummond House,* 17 Drummond Place. Telephone: 0131-225-1101. 3 rooms. New Town charmer with canopied beds and antique furniture.

Edinburgh, *No. 22 Murrayfield Gardens,* Tim and Christine MacDowel. Telephone: 0131-337-3569. Fax: 0131-337-3803. E-mail: No22forbandb@dial.pipex.com. A large Victorian house in a quiet residential neighborhood, No. 22 boasts an especially handsome drawing room. The pleasant dining room overlooks lovely gardens.

Edinburgh, *24 Northumberland Street,* 24 Northumberland Street. Telephone: 0131-556-8140. Fax: 0131-556-4423. E-mail: ingram@ednet.co.uk. 3 rooms, most ensuite. Classic Georgian townhouse a few minutes' walk from Princes Street and Waverley Station. Features period decoration with antique furnishings.

Edinburgh, *17 Abercromby Place,* Eirlys Smith, 17 Abercromby Place. Telephone: 0131-557-8036. Fax: 0131-558-3453. E-mail: eiryls.lloyd@virgin.net. 9 rooms, all ensuite. Historic Georgian house; formerly the home of Edinburgh architect William Playfair. Handsome, elegant, the epitome of New Town style. Two of the nicest rooms are located on the upper floor at the back of the main house. Comfortable dining room and sitting rooms too.

Edinburgh, *Turret Guest House,* Jackie and Ian Cameron, 8 Kilmaurs Terrace. Telephone: 0131-667-6704. Fax: 0131-668-1368. 3 rooms. This Victorian guesthouse is located in a quiet part of town. Among its notable features are a wooden staircase, attractive and neat bedrooms, and unusual breakfasts (haggis has been known to appear on the menu).

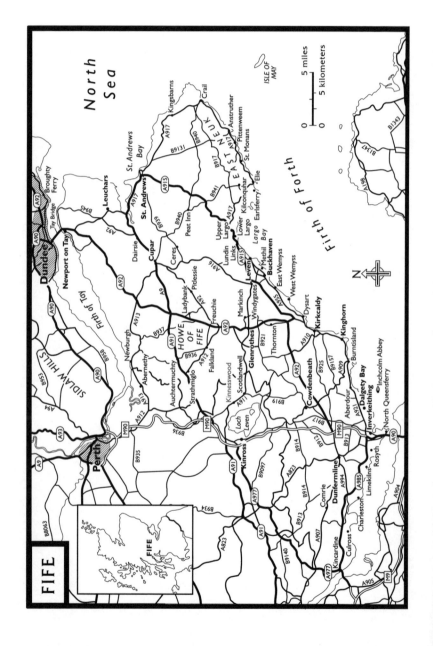

FIFE

Fife

"The Kingdom of Fife" has a nice ring to it. More than just an attractive moniker though, the name signifies the important position that the region held in earlier times, first as the seat of early Celtic kings in Dunfermline and later as the ecclesiastical capital in St. Andrews.

Nowadays most people associate Fife not with dead monarchs and clerics but rather with golf, charming fishing villages, and a great and ancient university.

The list of attractions to see and things to do in St. Andrews is considerable. Founded in 1410-11, St. Andrews University is the oldest university in Scotland—its buildings are scattered throughout the town, and students offer guided tours of the university during the summer months.

For many years St. Andrews was considered an important center of pilgrimage. St. Andrews Museum offers a solid introduction to the city's ecclesiastical, academic, and civic history, as well as a fascinating exhibit on the medieval pilgrims. After digesting the historical highlights, make your way to the ruins of St. Andrews Cathedral and the 100-foot St. Rule's Tower.

Of course, St. Andrews wouldn't be St. Andrews without golf. Every golfer's dream is to play at the Royal and Ancient Golf Club, the home of golf. If your skill level doesn't quite match your ambition, no matter. You can learn everything you've always wanted to know about golf—and more—at the very informative British Golf Museum. Of course, it's only a few steps from the Royal and Ancient.

In Fife the sea is never too far away. Discover its maritime history at the Scottish Fisheries Museum in Anstruther. Or better yet get a taste of the sea itself by visiting the East Neuk of Fife, which consists of a string of attractive fishing villages from Earlsferry to Crail. Further south in tiny Dysart sits a cluster of seventeenth-century fisher houses, complete with crowstep gables, that huddle around the picturesque old harbor.

Inland Fife has its share of attractive villages too, such as tony Falkland. My vote for the prettiest village in the area, though, goes to Culross (pronounced "COO-rus"), with its red roofs and narrow cobblestoned streets. Although it may look like a museum piece, it really is a viable community. You could easily spend an entire day here exploring the nooks and crannies of the village or visiting the numerous museums and historic buildings. Don't forget to stop by the impressive thirteenth-century Culross Abbey.

The Smugglers Inn
Neil and Christine Park
High Street
Anstruther
Telephone: 01333-310506
Fax: 01333-312706
E-mail: smugglers@norscot.idps.co.uk
Bedrooms: 8 rooms, all ensuite.
Rates: £29.50 pp. **Credit cards:** VISA, MasterCard, Switch, Solo. **Open:**
Year-round. **Children:** Well-behaved children are welcome regardless
of age. **Pets:** By arrangement. **Smoking:** Yes, but courtesy is expected.
Provision for handicapped: No. **Directions:** From Edinburgh go to
dual carriageway joining the M90. Exit the M90 at Junction 2
(Kirkcaldy-Glenrothes). Stay on this road until you come to a roundabout. Take the third exit (City Centre-St. Andrews). Continue on this
road until you reach the village of Anstruther. The inn is situated on
the right just past the "bad bend."

The original inn dates back to 1300. In the days of Queen Anne,
during the eighteenth century, it functioned as a tavern and even had
some historical associations with the Jacobite Rising of 1715. The inn
overlooks the harbor on the River Forth and is surrounded by some
of the best golf courses in Scotland, as well as many fine beaches.
Pleasantly decorated, it offers a comfy lounge with log fires. The neat
and attractive whitewashed building with black trim sports a rustic
look. Family-run, the Parks will take good care of you. If you have
the time, wander along the old streets of Anstruther. A "must stop"
is the Scottish Fisheries Museum on the harbor, which is housed in a
cluster of historic buildings around a cobbled courtyard. This fine
museum covers virtually all aspects of Scotland's fishing history, from
fisherfolk life to fishing tragedies.

Caiplie Guest House
Sandy and Sandra Strachan
53 High Street
Crail
Telephone/Fax: 01333-450564
Bedrooms: 7 rooms, 3 ensuite.
Rates: From £17. **Credit cards:** None. **Open:** March-November.
Children: Yes. **Pets:** By arrangement. **Smoking:** Yes. **Provision for handicapped:** No. **Directions:** Located along Crail's main street, about 10 miles south of St. Andrews.

This comfortable and casual Victorian guesthouse is run by the Strachan family. Some of the rooms offer wonderful sea views. What's more, the very reasonable accommodations, combined with tasty home cooking, make this a great bargain. Another advantage is the guesthouse's enviable location in the heart of the atmospheric fishing village of Crail, the most easterly of the fishing villages located in the East Neuk of Fife. The town's stone-built vernacular architecture, red pantile roofs, steeped gables, and narrow winding streets are so characteristic of the area. Ask the Strachans, a very accommodating couple, for their recommendations about things to do in the area. Best of all though, the Caiplie has an excellent reputation for good, home-cooked meals. Every meal is cooked to order.

Dundonald Arms Hotel
Michael Batchelor
Mid Causeway
Culross
Telephone/Fax: 01383-881137
Bedrooms: 7 rooms, all ensuite.
Rates: £40 per room (breakfast is extra here: a light breakfast goes
for £4.50, a full breakfast for £7). **Credit cards:** VISA and MasterCard.
Children: All ages. **Pets:** Restricted. **Smoking:** Yes. **Provision for hand-
icapped:** Limited to ground floor. **Directions:** Located in the heart of
Culross, which is located on the western edges of Fife.

The Dundonald is a grand old building located in the heart of the
historic village of Culross. The present building dates back to 1640
and over the centuries has offered many a visitor shelter, food, and a
wee dram. "Rumor has it," says Michael, the proprietor, "that a few
friendly spirits have remained from yesteryear; no doubt still enjoying the friendly company of today's visitors and the locals who use
our bars for the odd refreshment." The Dundonald has two eating and
drinking areas: the Top Bar functions as the village's meeting area and
has a nautical theme. It also has a fine selection of malt whiskies.
Whisky is also the theme of the Quaich Lounge, and prints of old
Culross decorate its walls. Also on the premises is Jackie's Gift Shop.
A piece of trivia: a tunnel passes under the gift shop floor which, in
earlier times, was used by monks who lived in the village and later by
smugglers. In good weather you can sit outside by the old Stables and
relax, and dream if you wish, in this quiet and utterly charming part of
Scotland. For those with more active interests, several golf courses
are within a short drive, and sailing can be arranged at South
Queensferry, about eight miles away. Whether staying overnight or just
stopping by for a pint, the staff at the Dundonald Arms is unfailingly
friendly and welcoming.

**The Albany Hotel &
  Garden Restaurant**
Antonio and Celia Ferraro
56 North Street
St. Andrews
Telephone: 01334-477737
Fax: 01334-477742
Bedrooms: 21 rooms, all ensuite. **Rates:** £55 per person. **Credit cards:** MasterCard, VISA, Delta, Diners Club, American Express, Switch. **Open:** Year-round. **Children:** Yes. **Pets:** No. **Smoking:** In smoker's lounge only. **Provision for handicapped:** No. **Directions:** Located near the ruins of St. Andrews Cathedral.

This Georgian townhouse, circa 1795, has been converted by the Ferraros to a small family-run hotel. From the moment you arrive at the Albany, you can't help but be won over by its combination of restful tranquility and a genuine effort to please its guests. It also doesn't hurt that the owners have a wonderful sense of humor and, after 15 years of marriage, offer playful jabs at each other's expense for the benefit of their guests. Antonio is originally from Naples, and Celia is a native of St. Andrews. They met in Monte Carlo and eventually made their way to St. Andrews, a fortunate circumstance for visitors to the city. The rooms are bright, cheery, and clean. One room called the Den, which faces away from street noise, has its own private garden and offers a soothing respite from the real world. There is a resident's bar with log fire and small library. The on-premises Garden Restaurant serves food with a Mediterranean flair. The Ferraros can also help organize golf outings, nights at the theatre, or tours of the area.

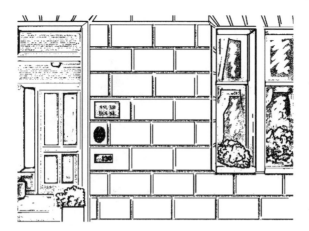

Aslar Guest House
Jean and Arlen Pardoe
120 North Street
St. Andrews
Telephone: 01334-473460
Fax: 01334-477540
E-mail: pardoe@aslar.u-net.com
Bedrooms: 5 rooms, all ensuite.
Rates: £25-30 pp. **Credit cards:** VISA and MasterCard. **Open:** Year-round. **Children:** All ages. **Pets:** No. **Smoking:** Restricted. **Provision for handicapped:** No. **Directions:** From Edinburgh take the road to the Forth Bridge/M90/A91. Follow the main road into St. Andrews, which becomes North Street.

The Pardoes started their career in the hospitality business in a modest way, back when their family was still young. Eventually they wished to try greater challenges, and so when an old house on North Street became available they "bit the bullet." The building dates from 1865 and was constructed on the site of a former coach house. Twenty years later it was purchased by a professor of Divinity and Biblical Criticism at nearby St. Andrews University. The Pardoes bought the property in 1985 and began major renovations, including removal of old and very heavy stone baths. It took several years for additional upgrading before Jean and Arlen were satisfied. ("We froze for the first winter without central heating," they say now). The result is a comfortable and modern dwelling, but one that also retains vestiges of its considerable past. The Aslar is a charming place by any standard.

Glenderran
Chris and Claire Toll
9 Murray Park
St. Andrews
Telephone: 01334-477951
Fax: 01334-477908
E-mail: glenderran@telinco.com
Bedrooms: 5 rooms, all ensuite. **Rates:** £26-45 double. **Credit cards:**
Delta, VISA, MasterCard, Switch. **Open:** Year-round. **Children:** Over
12. **Pets:** No. **Smoking:** No. **Provision for handicapped:** No.
Directions: Enter St. Andrews on the A91 road. On entering town go
straight over the first roundabout and then straight over the next
mini-roundabout (rather than turning right). Turn into Murray Place,
by the Tudor Inn. Follow the road round and turn right into Murray
Park (a one-way street).

This small late-Victorian guesthouse is centrally located just a few
hundred yards from the Old Course, beach, town center, and the university. It's run by Chris and Claire Toll, who specialize in customized
and friendly service. Consider some of their thoughtful details:
Individual bottles of mineral water are freshly supplied each day, and
in addition to the usual color remote-control television, they have
added a CD/cassette/radio player with a selection of CDs provided.
Each room is individually and tastefully decorated. Their largest
room, the Superior room, includes a three-seat sofa, 26-inch television
and video player, and such original Victorian features as elaborate ceiling work, marble fireplace, and bay windows. A full Scottish breakfast

or, for those with lighter appetites, a continental breakfast, is served. There's always a selection of cheeses, smoked salmon with scrambled egg, or vegetarian dishes on the menu. The dining room lounge is perfect for relaxing and meeting with friends or having a drink. There's also a good range of single malts, as well as a selection of books, CDs, and board and card games.

Montague House
Robb and Susan Swimm
21 Murray Park
St. Andrews
Telephone: 01334-479287
Fax: 01334-475827
E-mail: montague@easynet.co.uk
Web site: www.scoot.co.uk/montaguehouse
Bedrooms: 7 rooms on 3 floors, all ensuite. **Rates:** £30 pp. **Credit cards:** VISA, MasterCard. **Open:** February-November. **Children:** Yes. **Pets:** Yes. **Smoking:** Non-smoking bedrooms; smoking in lounge only. **Provision for handicapped:** No. **Directions:** Murray Park is a one-way street located off St. Andrews' main road.

This modernized Victorian terrace is located in the heart of town, minutes away from the Old Course. Rooms are individually decorated, with beautiful murals located throughout the house. Robb and Susan have an interesting story of their own to tell. They met in Vail, Colorado, and having lived there for about half a dozen years ("It is a great place to live when you love to ski as much as Robb does!" says Susan), decided to return to Britain. Robb had just graduated from Johnson and Wales University in Providence, Rhode Island, as a hotel and restaurant hospitality major. Susan had spent her childhood in St. Andrews. Robb and Susan, who took over Montague in June 1997, pride themselves on good food and maintaining a friendly and comfortable atmosphere with first-class service. They can arrange special trips, golf times, and dinner reservations. Breakfasts at Montague House are special occasions, from a traditional Scottish breakfast to more unusual items such as pancakes (a rare breakfast item in Scotland) and vegetarian dishes. The murals truly set the Montague apart. Each room is unique: five contain hand-painted murals and trompe l'eoil work done by local artist Gregor Gall, who is now living in Barcelona ("he is an old friend of mine and is extremely clever with a paint brush," says Susan); the nautically-themed Beachcomber has portholes painted on the walls; smothered in antique golf prints, the Bunker features a handpainted shelf on the wall and golf tees, sweets, and things painted on the window ledge; the Conservatory has an "amazing" ceiling that is painted like the sky; and the Secret Garden is a small but pretty pink room. There used to be a window overlooking the garden, until the previous owners built an extension. Robb and Susan have painted a garden in the dummy window and installed a window seat. Although Ceol-na-mara, the largest room with its king- and queen-size beds, has no murals, it does offer a Scottish theme in soothing plum colors. There is also a view of the East Neuk mural in the lounge and another mural on the half landing.

ALSO RECOMMENDED

Anstruther, *The Spindrift,* Pittenweem Road. Telephone: 01333-310573. Fax: 01333-310573. E-mail: spindrift@east-neuk.co.uk.
8 rooms, 7 ensuite. Located on the western edge of the East Neuk fishing village of Anstruther, the Spindrift is ideal for golf, touring, or just relaxing and taking in the sites of this lovely corner of Fife.

Crail, *Selcraig House,* Margaret Carstairs, 47 Nethergate. Telephone: 01333-450697. 5 rooms. Centuries-old stone house, warm and relaxing, with Edwardian theme. Small garden in the back.

Dunfermline, *Clarke Cottage Guest House,* 139 Halbeath Road. Telephone: 01383-735935. 9 rooms, all ensuite. This handsome nineteenth-century Victorian stone house is close to the town center. Guests can enjoy a separate entrance as well as ample off-street parking.

Dysart, *White Gates,* Tim and Ellis Musson, 91 Norman Road. Telephone: 01592-653337. 2 rooms; 1 ensuite, 1 shared. Victorian house with spacious bedrooms in the historic and lovely town of Dysart.

Kingsbarns, *Cambo House,* Mr. P. Erskine. Telephone: 01333-450313. Fax: 01333-450987. 2 rooms, 1 ensuite. Wooded coastal estate near St. Andrews. Features gardens, grounds, and fourposter beds; near woodlands and sandy beaches.

Kirkcaldy, *Arboretum,* Elizabeth Duncan, 20 Southerton Road. Telephone: 01592-643673. 2 rooms, both ensuite. Extended bungalow overlooking leafy Beveridge Park. Short walk to rail and bus stations and town center.

Leslie, *The Coach House,* David Morrison, Auchmuirbridge, near Glenrothes. Telephone/Fax: 01592-744934. 4 rooms, all ensuite. Beautiful white stucco home with red-tiled roof in a lovely part of rural Fife. Comfortably furnished, there are also plenty of outdoor activities to choose from: walking on the Lomond Hills, golf, shooting, fishing, and horseback riding.

Markinch, *Gamekeeper's Cottage,* Sam and Lesley Millar, Balbirnie Park. Telephone: 01592-612742. 2 rooms, both ensuite. Original gamekeeper's cottage. Gamekeeper's is known for its delicious home cooking. The motto of the Millars is simple: "Drive Carefully, Get Here Safely, and We'll Do the Rest." What more could you ask for?

By **Markinch,** *Shythrum Farm,* Mrs. C. Craig. Telephone: 01592-758372. 2 rooms, 1 ensuite. Small B&B with red slate roof and plenty of historic charm.

St. Andrews, *Annandale Guest House,* Brian and Florence McAndie, 23 Murray Park. Telephone/Fax: 01334-475310. 5 rooms, all ensuite. Lovely Victorian house. Golf times can be arranged.

St. Andrews, *Dunvegan Hotel,* Jack and Sheena Willoughby, 7 Pilmour Place. Telephone: 01334-473105. Fax: 01334-479102. 5 rooms, all ensuite. Recently renovated. The on-site Claret Jug Restaurant specializes in chargrilled steaks. Your American and Scottish hosts Jack and Sheena are known for their personal and friendly service. Dunvegan is located "only a 9-iron" from the Old Course. The golf-oriented lounge bar features over 40 prints of Old Course shots.

St. Andrews, *11 Queens Gardens,* Muriel Gray. Telephone: 01334-475536. 3 rooms, 1 ensuite. Elegant Victorian family home in the heart of the historic center of town. Attractive bedrooms. All major attractions within walking distance.

Near **St. Andrews,** *Little Carron Cottage,* Mrs. A. Finn, Little Carron Gardens. Telephone: 01334-474039. Fax: 01334-474039. 3 rooms, all ensuite. Attractive converted farmhouse in rural area. Each room has its own private lounge. Quiet, informal, friendly atmosphere. Excellent breakfasts.

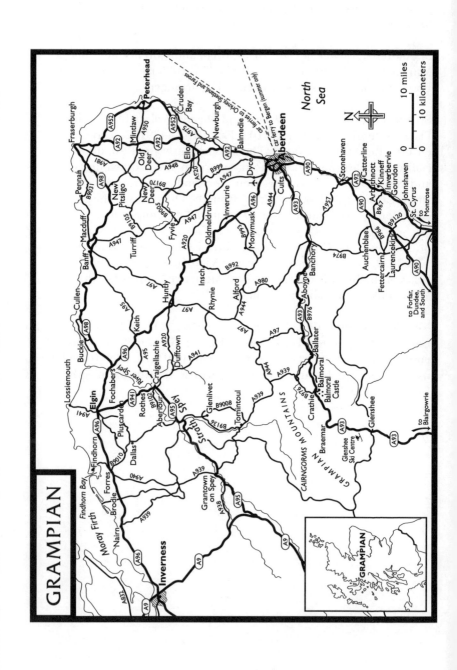

GRAMPIAN

North Sea

N

10 miles

10 kilometers

Peterhead

Fraserburgh

Cruden Bay

Newburgh

Balmedie

Aberdeen

Cults

Dyce

car ferry to Bergen (summer only)

or ferries to Orkney, Shetland and Faeroes

Stonehaven

Catterline

Kinneff

Inverbervie

Gourdon

Johnshaven

St. Cyrus

to Montrose

Mintlaw

Old Deer

New Deer

Ellon

Pennan

New Pitsligo

Oldmeldrum

Inverurie

Monymusk

Auchenblae

Fettercairn

Laurencekirk

Banff

Macduff

Fyvie

Turriff

Insch

Huntly

Rhynie

Alford

Aboyne

Banchory

to Forfar, Dundee, and South

Cullen

Keith

Dufftown

Lossiemouth

Buckie

Craigellachie

Aberlour

Rothes

Fochabers

Elgin

Pluscarden

Dallas

Findhorn

Strath Spey

Glenlivet

River Spey

Tomintoul

Ballater

Crathie

Balmoral

Balmoral Castle

Braemar

Glenshee

Glenshee Ski Centre

CAIRNGORMS MOUNTAINS

GRAMPIAN MOUNTAINS

to Blairgowrie

Findhorn Bay

Forres

Brodie

Nairn

Grantown on Spey

Moray Firth

Inverness

GRAMPIAN

Grampian

Castles, malt whisky trails, and fishing villages are just some of the better-known attractions of rural Grampian. Add to this the urban site of Aberdeen, Scotland's great maritime city, and you have an unusual combination. The Northeast also boasts a very rich folk tradition, from the colorful local dialects to the old ballads that are so greatly associated with this part of Scotland.

Aberdeen is the third-largest city in Scotland and, by dint of the silver granite buildings, one with an unusually distinctive look and feel. From Provost Skene's House, the oldest house in Aberdeen, to the icicle-like spires of magnificent Marischal College, Aberdeen looks like no other city in Scotland.

Founded as a royal burgh in 1124, Aberdeen developed into an important maritime center from its earliest days. You can discover more about its seaworthy past at the Aberdeen Maritime Museum, which explores everything from the days of the old clipper ships to the current spate of activity associated with the burgeoning oil industry. If you have time, try to visit lovely Old Aberdeen, a compact neighborhood of old stone cottages and cobblestoned streets and home to the campus of the University of Aberdeen. Several fine old churches are also here, including King's College Chapel and St. Machar's Cathedral. And don't forget the city's lively nightlife. Seek out the Lemon Tree for the latest sounds.

Rural Aberdeenshire is a world apart from the bustle of Aberdeen. It is a region of rolling hills, miles upon miles of woodland, and farming communities. The landscape is surprisingly diverse, from the fertile red soil of the interior to evocative fishing villages, including St. Cyrus, Johnshaven, Gourdon, and Stonehaven. While here you must order fish and chips at the Bervie Chipper in Inverbervie, a bustling and popular spot that has won numerous dining awards. Indeed, more than a few people insist that the Chipper serves the best fish and chips in Britain. I'll leave that distinction up to you.

Vast portions of Grampian seem terribly remote. The road to Braemar is as wild as any Highland glen. Royal Deeside, a favorite haunt of the royal family since Queen Victoria "discovered" the area in the 1840s, consists of delightful villages—pleasant Banchory, pretty Ballater, and subtly elegant Braemar.

And then there's the Malt Whisky Trail—Glenfarclas, Glenfiddich, Glenlivet, Macallan, Tamnavulin. Some of the names may sound familiar; others less so. Many of the distilleries have visitor's centers and offer free "wee drams." Proceed with caution though, especially if you're the driver.

Schiehallion House
Julie and Steven Heyes
Glenshee Road
Braemar
Telephone: 01339-741679
Bedrooms: 9 rooms, 5 ensuite.
Rates: £19-21. **Credit cards:** Access, VISA. **Open:** February-mid-September. **Children:** No. **Pets:** By arrangement. **Smoking:** In guest lounge only. **Provision for handicapped:** No. **Directions:** From the Mews in the village center, turn right. At road junction go south on A93 for 300 meters. Schiehallion is on the right.

This small stone-built B&B in the pretty village of Braemar is an all-family affair and a short walk from the village center. Schiehallion operates under the caring and watchful eyes of Julie and Steve and Steve's parents Sheila and Fred. The Heyes moved from the north of England to Braemar in June 1995 to, "get away from the rat race," as they say. Packed lunches are available on request. Evening meals can be had next door at the Braemar Lodge Hotel. The rooms are attractive and the resident's lounge welcoming with its open fire. The village itself is a wonderful base for exploring the surrounding countryside. Within a short drive of the B&B are such attractions as Balmoral Castle, the royal family's summer quarters since the days of Queen Victoria; the wild delights of the Cairngorm Mountains; and a series of charming villages along the A93 from Ballater to Banchory. Don't miss the chance to explore Braemar itself, which is an utterly delightful village with many quality shops. The Braemar Gallery, for example, specializes in Scottish art, paintings, sculptures, etchings, and drawings.

ALSO RECOMMENDED

Aberdeen, *Aberdeen Springdale Guest House,* Ms. F. Stirling, 404 Great Western Road. Telephone: 01224-316561. Fax: 0124-210773. 6 rooms, some with private facilities. Warm and cozy Victorian house with spacious rooms.

Ballater, *The Green Inn Restaurant with Rooms,* Jeff and Carol Purves, 9 Victoria Road. Telephone/Fax: 013397-55701. 3 rooms, all ensuite. The Green Inn is located in the center of the village, overlooking the village green. This two-story granite building offers modern Scottish cooking with international touches prepared to utmost perfection in its intimate dining room.

Ballater, *Netherley Guest House,* 2 Netherley Place. Telephone: 013397-55792. Pretty guesthouse overlooking Ballater's village green.

Johnshaven, *The Retreat,* Christine Hulton, South Street. Telephone: 01561-362731. 2 rooms, 1 ensuite. Tranquility by the sea. The tiny fishing village of Johnshaven is undeniably delightful all its own. Everything here is on a small scale, which seems only right.

By **Stonehaven,** *Lairhillock Inn & Restaurant,* Frank and Anne Budd, Netherley. Telephone: 01569-730001. Fax: 01569-731175.
E-mail: lairhillock@lairhillock.force9.co.uk. 2 rooms. Traditional small inn with restaurant. Originally a farmhouse, it features modern Scottish cooking imaginatively prepared. Suitably rustic—low ceilings, log fires, and whatnot—Lairhillock is also blessed with a friendly and efficient staff.

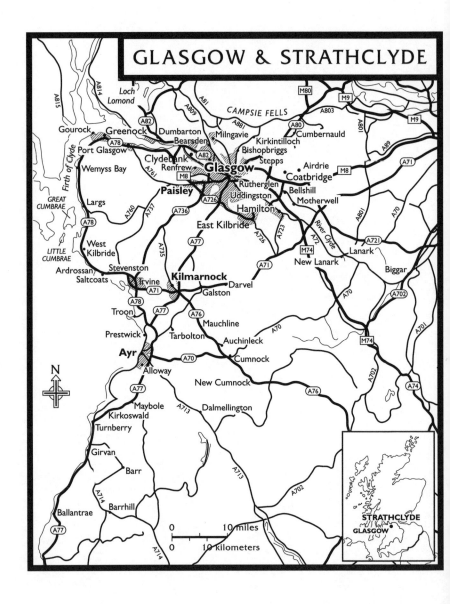

GLASGOW & STRATHCLYDE

A815 A814 Loch Lomond A82 A81 M80 M9 M9

CAMPSIE FELLS A803 A801

Gourock A809 A881 A80 Cumbernauld A89

Greenock Dumbarton Milngavie Kirkintilloch

A78 Bearsden Bishopbriggs A71

Port Glasgow A82 Stepps Airdrie M8

Wemyss Bay Clydebank Renfrew Glasgow Coatbridge

M8 A761 Paisley Rutherglen Bellshill

GREAT CUMBRAE A726 Uddingston Motherwell

Largs A760 A737 A736 Hamilton A70

A78 East Kilbride A736 A723 A72 A721

LITTLE CUMBRAE A77 A71 New Lanark Lanark

A735 M74 Biggar

Stevenston A71 Kilmarnock A71 A70 A702

Ardrossan Saltcoats Irvine Darvel

A78 A71 Galston

Troon A77 A76 A70 M74

Prestwick Mauchline A701

Ayr Tarbolton Auchinleck

Alloway A70 Cumnock A702

A77 New Cumnock A76 A74

Maybole A713 Dalmellington

Kirkoswald

Turnberry

Girvan A713

Barr A702

A714

Ballantrae Barrhill

A77 A714

Firth of Clyde
West Kilbride
River Clyde

N

0   10 miles
0   10 kilometers

STRATHCLYDE
GLASGOW

Glasgow & Strathclyde

If you had told a native of Glasgow a dozen or so years ago that the "dear green place," the city's nickname, would be in the throes of a major cultural renaissance, you would have been treated with wails of delirious laughter.

Who's laughing now?

Make no mistake about it: Scotland's largest city is enjoying a cultural epiphany unlike anything it has experienced in its history. Ever since it won the coveted European City of Culture status in 1990, the city has never looked back. And unlike its more conservative rival to the east, Edinburgh, Glasgow has never been afraid to take risks. After all, this is the city of Charles Rennie Mackintosh, that indisputable genius of architecture and design who was decades ahead of his time. From the ultramodern "Armadillo" (actually the Clyde Auditorium), which recalls the sleek sophistication of the Sydney Opera House, to Mackintosh's own Glasgow School of Art, Glasgow's city streets are awash with new and old landmarks.

In 1999 Glasgow earned yet another accolade: U.K. City of Architecture and Design. To celebrate its architectural heritage the city welcomed a new addition to the skyline. The Lighthouse, a $19.6 million restoration of the old *Glasgow Herald* building located in Mitchell Lane off Buchanan Street, opened during the summer of 1999, to much anticipation. The first major building designed by Mackintosh, the revamped structure is reportedly Europe's largest center for design and architecture. It contains an interpretation center on Mackintosh's life and work, permanent exhibits, a 100-seat conference room, and a café.

Other important Mackintosh sites in the city include the Willow Tea Room on Sauchiehall Street, House for an Art Lover in Bellahouston Park, and the Mackintosh House at the Hunterian Art Gallery, on the campus of the University of Glasgow.

The most popular attraction in Glasgow remains the always-impressive Burrell Collection, which houses over 8,000 objects under a glass roof in a leafy section of the city. Meanwhile, in the center of town, the Gallery of Modern Art contains four floors devoted to the work of living artists from throughout the world.

The Tenement House is a typical Victorian tenement flat circa 1892. Once the home of an ordinary Glasgow shorthand typist, who lived here for more than 50 years, the house has been turned into a fascinating living history museum of sorts.

If you want to learn more about the lives of ordinary Glaswegians, a visit to the People's Palace in Glasgow Green is essential. The Palace, which celebrated its 100th anniversary in January 1998, contains all kinds of artifacts and mementos connected with the lives of ordinary Glasgow men and women. It's fun, informative, and, best of all, free!

But there's also an older Glasgow to explore as well. Within the Cathedral District on the east side of town, once the center of civil and ecclesiastical government in Glasgow, stands dark and gaunt Glasgow Cathedral. One of the finest examples of Gothic architecture in Scotland, here you will find the tomb of St. Mungo, or Kentigern, Glasgow's patron saint. Also in the district and definitely worth a sustained visit is the St. Mungo Museum of Religious Life and Art, reportedly the only museum of its kind in the world.

Babbity Bowster
Fraser Laurie
16-18 Blackfriars Street
Glasgow
Telephone: 0141-552-5055
Fax: 0141-552-7774
Bedrooms: 6 rooms, all ensuite.
Rates: From £50 double. **Credit cards:** MasterCard/Eurocard, American Express, VISA. **Open:** All year except Christmas Day and New Year's Day. **Children:** All ages. **Pets:** Yes. **Smoking:** Yes. **Provision for handicapped:** No. **Directions:** Located in the Merchant City between George Street and Argyle Street.

With a name like Babbity Bowster, you know you're in for something unusual. Located in the Merchant City, as the fashionable East End of the city is now called, the Bowster is an old building. Designed by noted Scot architect James Adam in 1792, it underwent a major facelift in 1985. It is said to be located on the site of a former monastery and at one point in its past was a coffeehouse frequented by the Tobacco Lords, who made their fortune in the American colonies during pre-Revolutionary days. The unusual name is reportedly taken from a dance called "the babbity bowster," "babbity" meaning "bob at the" and "bowster" meaning large pillow. Today it is a popular combination café, bar, hotel, and restaurant. The Babbity consists of three levels. The bedrooms are located on the top floor; the Schottische restaurant and dining room is on the second floor, and the pub and café are on the ground level. Meals in the baronial Schottische Restaurant upstairs are served on round and oval wooden tables. In the evening the restaurant adopts a more romantic and sophisticated mood, with candles glowing on each table. Breakfast is served here in the morning. The pub has an appropriately worn look, without being shabby. The food is filling, tasty, and nourishing; the attentive and gregarious young waitstaff are always ready to assist. Spend a few hours here in the evening and you're guaranteed to meet more than a few characters, from visiting musicians (music sessions are popular at the Babbity) to brainy schoolteachers on their way home after a long day in the classroom. Throughout it all, Fraser Laurie, the friendly movie-star-handsome owner with a patch over one eye, watches attentively. A happy observation: there are no televisions on the premises. With so many interesting specimens of humanity coming and going through the front door, how can you not be entertained?

Cathedral House
Mr. B. McAneny
28-32 Cathedral Square
Glasgow
Telephone: 0141-552-3519
Fax: 0141-552-2444
Bedrooms: 6 rooms with bath and shower, 2 rooms with shower.
Rates: £49 single, £69 double. **Credit cards:** VISA, American Express, Diners Club, MasterCard. **Open:** Year-round except Christmas and New Year's Day. **Children:** Yes. **Pets:** No. **Smoking:** Yes. **Provision for handicapped:** Only in café bar. **Directions:** From airport follow the M8 to Glasgow City Centre, taking the Glasgow Cathedral exit, which will take you to a set of traffic lights facing the Royal Infirmary. Follow the road to the right and turn left at the next set of lights. Cathedral House is the first building on the right.

Situated in the Cathedral District, in the medieval heart of old Glasgow, the Cathedral House is located just steps away from the thirteenth-century Glasgow Cathedral, the Provand's Lordship (the oldest house in Glasgow), and the Necropolis, a truly grand Victorian cemetery. The hotel itself has a colorful history. It was established in 1877 as a hostel by the Discharged Prisoners Aid Society and built in the Scottish baronial style. Restored in 1990, the hotel to this day remains faithful to the original design. There is an excellent upstairs restaurant that is unusual in another way—it is the only Icelandic restaurant in Glasgow, indeed perhaps in all of Scotland. Among its specialties include Scottish game, poultry, and fish. The meat and fish courses are cooked Icelandic style at the table. Local jazz, folk, and blues acts are regularly featured. All in all, Cathedral House is a friendly, down-to-earth historic gem.

Kirklee Hotel
Douglas and Rosemary Rogen
11 Kensington Gate
Glasgow
Telephone: 0141-334-5555
Fax: 0141-339-3828
E-mail: kirklee@clara.net
Web site: www.kirkleehotel.co.uk
Bedrooms: 9 rooms, all ensuite.
Rates: £64 double. **Credit cards:** VISA, MasterCard, American Express,
Diners Club. **Open:** Year-round except Christmas Eve and Christmas
Day. **Children:** Yes. **Pets:** No. **Smoking:** Yes. **Provision for handicapped:**
No. **Directions:** Take the Great Western Road (A82) to Horselethill
Road. Kensington Gate is the first on the right.

Set in Glasgow's West End, this gracious Edwardian lodging is full
of character and forms a part of Kensington Gate, a series of red sandstone townhouses. The Kirklee is situated away from the main roads
and overlooks a private park, so a restful night is assured. The terrace
was designed by David Barclay in 1902 and built in the grand style of
the townhouses of the era. You enter through a grand door and into a
paneled hallway. Period furniture and oil paintings by Scottish and
international artists add to the old-world atmosphere, as do the gold
and deep blue colors, carved fireplace, and original parquet floors. Tall
oriole windows overlook the private gardens. All rooms are individually
furnished with lovely fabrics and designs. Unlike most establishments,
breakfast is served in your room. The Rogens are a helpful couple who
do their best to make you feel at home. The Kirklee is a short walk from
the many restaurants and bars along busy Byres Road, the West End's
major thoroughfare. Opulent, dignified, and supremely civilized, the
Kirklee is a delight any way you look at it.

Nairns
Nick and Topher Nairns
13 Woodside Crescent
Glasgow
Telephone: 0141-353-0707
Fax: 0141-331-1684
E-mail: info@nairns.co.uk
Web site: www.nairns.co.uk
Bedrooms: 4 rooms, all ensuite.
Rates: From £90 to £125 per room. **Credit cards:** MasterCard/
Eurocard, American Express, VISA, Diners Club, Switch, Delta. **Open:**
Year-round except Christmas, Boxing Day (December 26), New Year's
Day, and January 2. **Children:** No. **Pets:** No. **Provision for handi-
capped:** No. **Directions:** From Charing Cross turn into Woodlands
Road, then take the first road on the left, Lynedoch Street, and then
make another left onto Lynedoch Terrace and still another left onto
Woodside Terrace. Woodside Crescent, located just off Sauchiehall
Street, is a continuation of Woodside Terrace.

Nairns is a converted townhouse located on a quiet Georgian crescent and only a 10-minute walk from Glasgow City center. It is perhaps
better known for its restaurant and its celebrity chef, Nick Nairns, who
is one of Scotland's most highly respected and deservedly popular
restaurateurs. Essentially Nairns is a five-star restaurant with rooms.
The restaurant takes up two floors. The formal dining room upstairs
serves sophisticated and innovative food to national and international
acclaim. (All of this luxury comes at a cost, of course). The downstairs eatery is more casual, with its modern dark benches and cool

grayish walls. As expected, the accommodations are just as ritzy. The Silver Room exudes, as its name indicates, a cool reserve, with steel bedposts. It's oh-so modern and minimalist. If Philip Glass were to design a hotel room, one imagines it would look like this. On the other side of the spectrum is the Amber Room, which projects a warm reddish glow. The Nantucket Room is done up in soft muted pale green; the striking bathroom, complete with red floor and red ceiling, includes a clawfooted tub. The "painterly" Vermeer Room features a trompe l'oeil effect. Sienna-colored doorways lead to the illusion of a balcony. Continental breakfast is extra at £7.50. A two-course lunch costs £13.50; a three-course, £17.

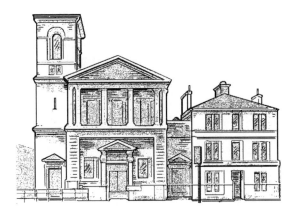

The Pipers' Tryst Hotel
A. G. Gordon
30-34 McPhater Street
Cowcaddens
Glasgow
Telephone: 0141-353-0220
Fax: 0141-353-1570
Bedrooms: 8 rooms, all ensuite.
Rates: £50 (special rates for students attending the piping school are available upon request). **Credit cards:** VISA. **Open:** Year-round.
Children: Yes. **Pets:** No. **Smoking:** Yes. **Provision for handicapped:** No. **Directions:** Located a short walk north of Sauchiehall Street, Glasgow's commercial center.

Built in 1873 and located in the theater district, the building has been spruced up and the interior thoroughly modernized. The Piper's Tryst opened in May 1996 as a combination bed and breakfast, café, and museum. The 8 rooms are comfortable and modern, without being too sterile. Extras include a trouser press and hair dryers. Complimentary continental breakfast can be served in your room at your request. If you wish to have a full Scottish breakfast, which includes generous helpings of bacon, fried eggs, tomatoes, sautéed potatoes, mushrooms, black pudding, potato scones, sausages, tea or coffee, and hot buttered toast for £3.50, make your way to the café. Downstairs is the National Museum of Piping, with its exhibits on the piping tradition, the music of the bagpipes, and the history of important piping families, including the most famous of all, the MacCrimmons of Skye. Among the items on display are various sets of pipes, from the Highland war pipes to the lesser-known Scottish small pipes. The center also contains a school with rehearsal rooms, a performance hall, reference library, conference facilities, and gift shop. Anyone who loves the pipes must stay here.

ALSO RECOMMENDED

Glasgow, *Albion Hotel,* 405-407 North Woodside Road. Telephone: 0141-339-8620. Fax: 0141-334-8159. 16 rooms, all ensuite. Located across from Kelvinbridge tube station in the heart of the West End.

Glasgow, *Hillview Guest House,* 18 Hillhead Street. Telephone: 0141-334-5585. Fax: 0141-353-3155. 10 rooms. Small and friendly West End guesthouse near the university and the Botanic Gardens.

Glasgow, *Kirkland House,* 42 St. Vincent Crescent. Telephone: 0141-248-3458. Fax: 0141-221-5174. E-mail: kirkland@gisp.net. 6 rooms, 3 ensuite. Family-owned guesthouse in the West End. Reasonable and neat. Great for all West End attractions.

Glasgow, *The Merchant Lodge* (formerly the Courtyard Hotel), 52 Virginia Street. Telephone: 0141-552-2424. Fax: 0141-552-4747. 34 rooms, all ensuite. Great value in the city center. This Merchant City accommodation is located in one of Glasgow's oldest buildings. Includes a cobblestoned courtyard and an old turnpike stair, one of the last in Glasgow still in use. Originally home to the city's Tobacco Lords. Near George Square, the City Chambers, Queen Street, and Central stations. Handsomely modern interior too: hardwood floors, pine furniture, and wicker chairs.

Glasgow, *Park House,* Mrs. D. Hallam, 13 Victoria Park Gardens South. Telephone: 0141-339-1559. Fax: 0141-576-0915. E-mail: xwf54@dial.pipex.com. 3 rooms, 2 ensuite. Handsome Victorian townhouse just 15 minutes from Glasgow Airport and 10 minutes from the city center.

Glasgow, *Scott's Guest House,* Kay and Bob Scott, 417 North Woodside Road. Telephone: 0141-339-3750. 8 rooms, all ensuite. This quiet guesthouse, just off busy Great Western Road in Glasgow's leafy West End, overlooks Kelvin Park. Peaceful.

Glasgow, *The Town House,* 4 Hughenden Terrace. Telephone: 0141-357-0862. Fax: 0141-339-9605. 20 rooms, all ensuite. Set back from busy Sauchiehall Street and blessed with its own private gardens, the Town House forms part of a tree-lined crescent of renovated Victorian townhouses.

Inverary, *Creagh Dhubh,* Richard and Janice MacLugash. Telephone: 01499-302430. 4 rooms, 1 ensuite. Handsome stone-built guesthouse with large garden located on the edge of town. Spacious rooms; some come with a loch view.

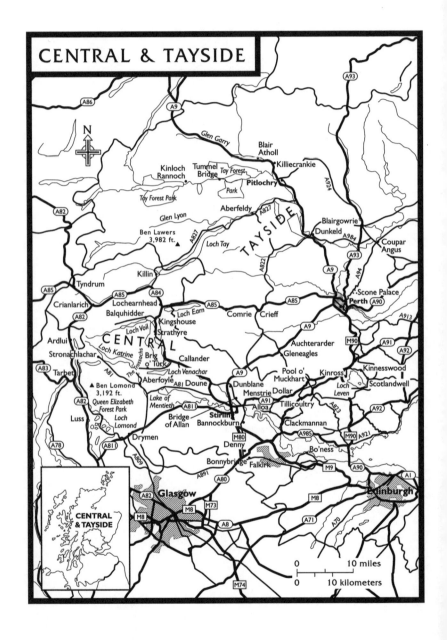

Central & Tayside

The focal point of the Scottish heartland converges in the old town of Stirling, once the Scottish capital and still a formidable place steeped in history and rife with atmospherics. Indeed, it has often been called Edinburgh in miniature.

The highlight of any visit to Stirling is a stop by Stirling Castle, that impenetrable fortress that looms high over the town, pondering the town's past and present like some watchful sentinel. From the castle take the time to admire the buildings of Stirling's Old Town. Nearby is the National Wallace Monument, an angular and distinctive landmark that can be seen from miles around.

A short distance from Stirling is the beauty of the Trossachs, that lush wooded paradise that has been attracting visitors since Sir Walter Scott first wrote about the area in the early nineteenth century. Among the many handsome towns and villages in the area include Callander, Aberfoyle, and Strathyre. The Rob Roy and Trossachs Visitor Centre in Callander is a good place to receive an introduction to the area, and a little bit about the legend and life of Rob Roy MacGregor, the Scottish folk hero whose colorful life was portrayed by Liam Neeson in the popular film *Rob Roy*.

The commercial heart of the area called Perthshire in the Tayside region is the handsome city of Perth. Three things helped to bring prosperity to Perth: salmon, wool, and whisky. And to that we might add tourism, for the visitor trade is placed quite high on the list of economic forces. Although Perth gained its royal burgh status in 1210, not much of old Perth remains. It looks very much a twentieth-century city, with the requisite upscale malls and shopping and substantial homes. But Perth also has its artistic side, being the home of the imposing Perth Museum and Art Gallery and the Perth Theatre.

The best-known theater festival in the region must belong to the Pitlochry Festival Theatre. Housed in a modern building that Prince

Charles officially dedicated on July 9, 1981, the theater is located on the south bank of the River Tummel with views of Ben y Vrackie beyond.

One of the most charming villages around is Dunkeld, once the ecclesiastical capital of Scotland. For such a small place, it has much to see. A short walk along Cathedral Street leads to the cathedral itself, a mixture of Gothic and Norman styles, which sits serenely on the banks of the River Tay. The cathedral is dedicated to St. Columba. According to tradition, his relics were buried under the chancel steps. Construction on the cathedral began in 1318, but the lovely structure was reduced to ruin during the Reformation. The choir, re-roofed in 1660, now serves as the parish church and is open daily. You will find a small museum in the fifteenth-century sacristy, which can be entered through the choir. The ruined fifteenth-century nave and tower are entrusted to the care of Historic Scotland.

Both Dunkeld and the adjacent Victorian village of Birnam are within walking distance of each other. Located in the center of Birnam is the Beatrix Potter Garden, which at first glance may seem an unusual place for a memorial to the creator of Peter Rabbit and other endearing childhood characters. Actually Potter had spent her childhood holidays here and drew inspiration from the area and its people for her Peter Rabbit tales.

Antique lovers need look no further than the indoor Scottish Antique & Arts Centre, near the tiny Perthshire village of Abernyte. Thirty dealers offer their antiques, art, rugs, pottery, furniture, and other wares. The centre is open seven days a week, from 10 A.M. to 5 P.M. There's also a lovely café on the premises.

Monachyle Mhor
Mrs. J. M. Lewis
Balquhidder
Lochearnhead
Perthshire
Telephone: 01877-384622
Fax: 01877-384305
E-mail: monachylemhorhotel@balquhidder.freeserve.co.uk
Bedrooms: 10 rooms, all ensuite.
Rates: £70-90 double. **Credit cards:** VISA, Access, Switch, MasterCard.
Open: All year. **Children:** 12 and older. **Pets:** No. **Smoking:** In bar only.
Provision for handicapped: Bar and restaurant only. **Directions:** 11
miles north of Callander on A84. Turn right at Kinghouse Hotel and
carry on up the glen road about four miles to Balquhidder.

Situated on their own 2,000 acres of land, the Lewis family runs both
the farming enterprise and the hotel that offers modern comfort with
the best of country living. One of the sons, Dick, runs the farm and is
the head shepherd; the older son, Tom, is head chef. Monachyle Mhor
was reportedly the first home of Rob Roy MacGregor, when the out-
law married at the age of twenty-one. Now it is a lovely small farmhouse
hotel located at the end of a long and winding road (and since it is
Scotland, of course, it is also a narrow one). The highly acclaimed
restaurant on the premises is known for its game and herbs taken from
the estate. The estate itself has magnificent views of Loch Voil and Loch
Doine. The handsome dining room sports salmon-colored walls and
oaken tables and chairs, along with old prints of blackface sheep and
cattle. The bedrooms are especially attractive, tastefully and imaginatively decorated. The Lewis's offer private salmon and trout fishing,
with red deer stalking and grouse shooting in season.

Arden House
Ian M. Mitchell and William R. Jackson
Bracklinn Road
Callander
Perthshire
Telephone/Fax: 01877-330235
Web site: www.smoothhound.co.uk/hotels/arden.html
Bedrooms: 6 rooms, all with private bath.
Rates: £25 pp. **Credit cards:** VISA, MasterCard, Delta. **Open:** March-November. **Children:** No children under 14. **Pets:** No. **Smoking:** No.
Provision for handicapped: 2 ground floor rooms. 5 steps at front of house. **Directions:** If traveling north by car leave the M9 motorway at Junction 10 north of Stirling, signposted to Crianlarich. Follow the A84 to Callander. In Callander turn right into Bracklinn Road before entering the village center. Arden House is 200 yards on the left.

Arden House stands in its own garden overlooking the attractive village of Callander, with wonderful views of nearby Ben Ledi and surrounding countryside. It's only a few minutes' walk from the village center. The house itself is a large Victorian stone-built dwelling with greenery on one side and woods at the rear. Two of the bedrooms are on the ground floor, as is the comfy sitting room. Callander, often called the gateway to the Trossachs, served as the model for the fictional Tannochbrae, made famous (throughout Britain at least) by the popular BBC television series *Dr. Finlay's Casebook*. Arden House was the television home of Drs. Finlay and Cameron and their housekeeper Janet. In addition to being only a two-minute walk from Callander's 18-hole golf course, Arden House is also close enough to enjoy the various summer cruises on Loch Lomond and Loch Katrine. Your hosts Ian and William not only "guarantee you a warm welcome to our home," the dynamic duo also serve fabulous full Scottish breakfasts.

The Pend
Peter and Marina Braney
5 Brae Street
Dunkeld
Telephone: 01350-727586
Fax: 01350-727173
E-mail: react@sol.co.uk
Web site: www.thepend.com
Bedrooms: 6 rooms, with private facilities.
Rates: £80 double (B&B and dinner); B&B only, £50 double. **Credit cards:** VISA, MasterCard, Eurocheque, Delta, JCB, American Express. **Children:** Yes; no charge for children up to 3 years. Children from 3 to 11 get half off. **Pets:** Yes. **Smoking:** In bedrooms and lounge only. **Provision for handicapped:** No. **Directions:** Located a short walk or drive up from Dunkeld Cathedral, just off Atholl Road, Dunkeld's commercial street.

Located up a hill off the main street of town and a short walk from Dunkeld Cathedral, the Pend sports a deceptively unassuming Georgian facade from the outside. But step inside and you'll be pleasantly surprised, for here you'll find six elegantly spacious rooms as well as a warm and friendly greeting from Peter and Marina (English and Irish, respectively) and their frisky Westie named Molly. Formerly a family home, the Braneys bought the property in 1997. "Our guests always come first," they say, and it shows. The rooms are furnished with many fine antiques. Each room comes equipped with a hand basin, luxury bathrobe, and color television. Although there are no ensuite facilities as of this writing, two large bathrooms are provided for the use of guests. Meals are served in the splendid sitting/dining room, beautifully decorated with its mustard walls and antique furniture. The four-course meal is something to behold and one that reflects the variety of fish, meat, game, fruit, vegetables, and cheeses of Perthshire. Breakfast is served when you want it—in other words, at the Pend you can sleep in without feeling guilty or pressured. Breakfast consists of a light selection (cereals, croissants, breads, fresh and preserved fruits) or a traditional Scottish breakfast but with a twist—scrambled eggs with local smoked salmon, Arbroath smokies (smoked haddock), porridge, and even haggis. Dietary needs can be accommodated as well. Guests of the Pend can use the leisure club facilities of the nearby Stakis Dunkeld House Hotel at discounted rates. Facilities include a heated indoor swimming pool, spa bath, sauna, steam room, multi-purpose gymnasium, tennis, croquet, putting, and archery. Also available are massage, beauty treatments, and a tanning salon. Enjoy the lovely walks along the River Tay and through the almost 200 acres of hotel grounds, which include a shooting range, salmon fishing, and mountain-bike rental. The Braneys are truly gracious people, and in the Pend you will enjoy one of the finest B&B experiences in all of Scotland. Tip: if possible, request the room at the top. It's quite a view.

Inverbeg Inn
Andrew D. Scott
Inverbeg
Near Luss
Telephone: 01436-860678
Fax: 01436-860686
E-mail: inverbeg@onyxnet.co.uk
Web site: www.scottish-selection.co.uk
Bedrooms: 19 rooms, all ensuite.
Rates: £35-45 double. **Credit cards:** VISA, American Express, MasterCard, Switch, Solo. **Open:** All year. **Children:** Yes. **Pets:** No. **Smoking:** Yes. **Provision for handicapped:** Yes. **Directions:** 3 miles north of Luss on the main route to the West Coast and the Mull of Kintyre. From Glasgow follow the signs for the Erskine bridge and then on to Loch Lomond along the A82.

One of the best-known small hotels in Scotland, the Inverbeg Inn is situated on the bonny banks of Loch Lomond, just beyond the tiny village of Luss. You couldn't ask for a better location. It's an area where truly breathtaking scenery, history, and culture come together. And if for some reason, and it's hard to imagine how, you ever tire of the many rural attractions, be assured that the thrills of big-city life—in this case, Glasgow—are only a short half hour away. The inn itself dates back to 1814. The lodge on the loch side looks east to Ben Lomond and Ben Vrakie. Each spacious room has its own individual character. With their warm yellow-tinged walls, the overall effect is of genuine good will. The inn specializes in local produce, including such tasty items as Loch Fyne oysters, scallops, salmon, Angus beef, Glen Finnart venison, and even herbs from the garden. Owner Andrew Scott always makes sure that an excellent range of single malt whiskies is always in stock.

The Lomond Country Inn
David Adams
Kinnesswood
By Loch Leven
Telephone: 01592-840253
Fax: 01592-840693
E-mail: the.lomond@dial.pipex.com
Web site: www.smoothhound.co.uk/
Bedrooms: 12 rooms, all ensuite.
Rates: £30 double. **Credit cards:** MasterCard/Eurocard, American Express, VISA, Diners Club, Switch, Delta. **Open:** Year-round. **Pets:** By arrangement. **Smoking:** Restricted. **Provision for handicapped:** Yes. **Directions:** Get off at Junction 5 on the M90 and follow signs for Scotlandwell. The Lomond Country Inn is located in the next village.

This friendly, reasonably priced, and cozy family-run hotel offers magnificent views over Loch Leven in the village of Kinnesswood. Of the 12 rooms, 4 are located in the inn itself and the other 8 are in a modern extension opposite. The Lomond Country Inn is within an hour's drive of 50-plus golf courses, as well as ample riding, walking, rambling, and birdwatching opportunities. In other words, this is peak outdoor country. If all this weren't enough, there are close to a dozen stillwater fisheries and four nearby rivers stocked with brown trout, rainbow trout, salmon, and sea trout. Cycling and walking paths are within close proximity, and in the summer there is a boat crossing to Loch Leven Castle, once the prison home of Mary Queen of Scots for over a year. The inn specializes in fresh seafood and freshwater fish, game, beef, lamb, vegetables, and seasonal fruit. The cost for a three-course dinner ranges from an affordable £10 to £14.

Craigroyston House
Douglas and Gretta Maxwell
2 Lower Oakfield
Pitlochry
Telephone/Fax: 01796-472053
Bedrooms: 8 rooms, all ensuite.
Rates: £20-28 per person. **Credit cards:** VISA, MasterCard. **Open:** Year-round except December. **Children:** Yes. **Pets:** No. **Smoking:** No smoking in bedrooms. **Provision for handicapped:** No. **Directions:** From Atholl Road, Pitlochry's main street, go past Bonnet Hill Road to East Moulin Road. From East Moulin Road turn onto Lower Oakfield Road.

Douglas Maxwell is a definite charmer, a natural salesman (and that is meant in the best sense of the word) who makes everyone who walks through his door feel at ease. He and his wife Gretta run their guest-house with gentle efficiency. Craigroyston is a short walk from the rail-way station, set in its own ground, and is located just off Pitlochry's main road. The bedrooms are spacious and elegant in an old-fash-ioned way. The cozy lounge boasts a log fire. Among the added touches that the Maxwells offer are drying, ironing, and shoe cleaning services. Outside Craigroyston's front door lies Pitlochry itself. Pitlochry started out as a tiny hamlet back in 1727. Now it's one of the most popular resort towns in Scotland. Take the time to walk along the main street, have a cup of tea and a sweet in its tearooms, or sim-ply window-shop at its many marvelous gift and woolen stores.

Ferryman's Cottage
Kath Sanderson
Port-Na-Craig
Pitlochry
Telephone: 01796-473681
Bedrooms: 2 rooms, 1 ensuite.
Rates: £18-20 single. **Credit cards:** No. **Open:** Closed November-Easter. **Children:** Yes. **Pets:** No. **Provision for handicapped:** No.
Directions: Two minutes from the A9, Ferryman's Cottage is situated below the Festival Theatre, the Dam and Fish Ladder, and by the suspension bridge below the theater.

The tiny historic hamlet of Port-Na-Craig was established about 300 years ago. The cottage functioned as the boat house before the bridge over the River Tummel was built to serve the resident population and cattle crossing the river. The cottage looks almost doll-like, sitting as it does by the river's edge. A riot of flowers adds color to the picture-postcard scene. Inside you'll find cozy and oh-so-comfy rooms, one ensuite, but all with color television and tea- and coffee-making facilities. A full Scottish breakfast is served in the compact dining room, which overlooks the River Tummel, renowned for its salmon. Port-Na-Craig is a short walk across the suspension bridge to Pitlochry. There is also a lovely garden and stone patio. The cottage is immediately adjacent to the Wee Kiosk ice cream stand, a temptation for those with a sweet tooth, especially during the height of summer.

Portnacraig Inn & Restaurant
Bill and Andrew Bryan
Portnacraig
Pitlochry
Telephone: 01796-472777
Bedrooms: 2 rooms, both ensuite.
Rates: £25 pp, ensuite. **Credit cards:** MasterCard/Eurocard, VISA, Switch, Delta. **Open:** Year-round. **Children:** Yes. **Pets:** Yes (well behaved). **Smoking:** Yes. **Provision for handicapped:** No. **Directions:** Located just over the suspension bridge in the tiny hamlet of Port-Na-Craig.

This lovely old stone inn on the banks of the River Tummel dates from circa 1650. It's located directly below the Pitlochry Festival Theatre. Although more of a restaurant than a bona fide inn—it only has two rooms after all—it's such an utterly charming place that I had to include it. The tiny windows of the bistro-style restaurant also overlook the river. The service is extremely friendly and very casual. If you're planning to attend a show at the festival theatre across the road you can dine alfresco (weather permitting of course) on the patio. And if the weather doesn't cooperate (this *is* Scotland), then you can take great pleasure in appreciating some of the nice touches found within the interior: low-beamed ceiling, green tablecloths, printed curtains, mauve-colored walls, and dark wooden chairs. The restaurant is open daily from 10 A.M.

Creagan House Restaurant with Accommodation
Gordon and Cherry Gunn
Strathyre
Near Callander
Telephone: 01877-384638
Fax: 01877-384319
Web site: www.milford.co.uk/go/creaganhouse.html
Bedrooms: 5 rooms, all ensuite.
Rates: £40. **Credit cards:** MasterCard, American Express, VISA. **Open:**
March to January. **Children:** Yes (children's tea served at 6 P.M. but no
one under 10 for dinner). **Pets:** Yes. **Smoking:** In lounge only. **Provision
for handicapped:** On ground-floor bedroom only. **Directions:** Located
along the A84, about .25 mile north of Strathyre.

The Gunns do their best to retain the simple charm of their seventeenth-century farmhouse. The location couldn't be better—a peaceful spot surrounded by lovely scenery. The tiny and charming village
of Strathrye is located at the head of Loch Lubnaig. Nearby are major
historical sites (Rob Roy's grave, Stirling Castle), yet Creagan House
seems far away from the rest of the world. Gordon and Cherry offer
five charming rooms (one with a fourposter bed) and many thoughtful extras thrown in. The Gunns bought Creagan in 1986, and they
run the B&B with their daughter Maria. Gordon has won accolades for
his cooking—variations on classical French cooking with Scottish
influences. They use fresh produce, much of it grown for them in
organic small holdings. Dinner is served amid the splendor of the
baronial dining hall. Two menus are offered: the menu of the day for
£18.50 and the "Chef's Favourite" at £22.50. A typical dinner may

consist of a warm plate of scallops, lobster, and crab with scallop roe sauce, or roast tomato and basil oil, followed by a choice of poached turbot on tarragon vegetables or spinach and pine nut-crusted rack of lamb with pear purée in a minted pea sauce or filet of venison with glazed sweet potato. For dessert, try the lemon and lime tart with passionfruit coulis, chocolate hazelnut mousse cake, or apple flapjack steamed pudding.

Fairfield Guest House
Mary Hunter
14 Princes Street
Stirling
Telephone: 01786-472685
Bedrooms: 6 rooms, all ensuite.
Rates: From £21. **Credit cards:** None. **Open:** March through October.
Children: All ages. **Pets:** By arrangement. **Smoking:** No. **Provision for handicapped:** No. **Directions:** From the Burghmuir roundabout at the entrance to Stirling, take the second left, passing the bus/railway station. At the roundabout at the railway station turn left into Station Road and then again at the first right at the mini-roundabout at the top of the road. Princes Street is the second left.

This long-established, family-run, and very tidy guesthouse boasts a wonderful location, located as it is just off the town center in a quiet residential cul-de-sac. Stirling Castle is but a short walk away, as are the other sites of the Old Town, including the Old Town Jail, the fifteenth-century Church of the Holy Rude, and Argyll's Lodging, once the residence of the earls, later dukes, of Argyll. Of course, there's plenty of opportunity within walking distance of fine shops and dining. As for the house itself, owner Mary Hunter runs a tight ship. Although only 100 years old (young by Scottish standards!), Fairfield is definitely full of character and period features, which is not to say that modern conveniences are given short shrift. On the contrary, everything appears appropriately contemporary and comfortably furnished. The exterior too is quite welcoming—a warm and mellow honey-colored two-story with a white door.

ALSO RECOMMENDED

Aberfoyle, *The Covenanters Inn,* Telephone: 01877-382347. Fax: 01877-382785. 5 single, 18 double, 24 twin, 5 family; all ensuite. Handsome country inn set on a wooded knoll overlooking the village. The inn is graced with singular details—oak beams, log fires, snug lounges—that add to its rustic appeal. Live entertainment is offered on several evenings each week throughout the year.

Aberfoyle, *Creag-Ard House,* Cara Wilson, Milton. Telephone: 01877-382297. 7 rooms, 4 ensuite. Lovely Victorian house nestled in three acres of gardens overlooking Loch Ard, with views to Ben Lomond beyond. Trout fishing and boating rentals can be arranged.

Aberfoyle, *The Forth Inn,* Phil and Tristan Crowder, Main Street. Telephone: 01877-382372. Fax: 01877-382488. E-mail: phil@for-thinn.com. 6 rooms, all ensuite. The Forth Inn is located on the main street of Aberfoyle, a pleasant holiday village with plenty of amenities—shops, museums, and outdoor activities, to name but a few—and loads of local character.

Birnam, *Waterbury Guest House,* Caroline and Brian Neil, by Dunkeld. Telephone: 01350-727324. Fax: 01350-727023. E-mail: bneil@waterbury.demon.co.uk. 8 rooms. This simple and clean Victorian guesthouse is located in the center of town, across the street from the Beatrix Potter Gardens. A nice local touch: listening to the music of Dougie Maclean at breakfast in the morning. Dougie runs the Dunkeld Records label and Maclean's Art and Music Gallery at the Taybank Hotel in Dunkeld.

Callander, *Riverview House,* Leny Road. Telephone: 01877-330635. 5 rooms, all ensuite. Victorian house set in its own grounds, within walking distance of shops and attractions.

Callander, *Bridgend Cottage,* Diana Hopper, Kilmahog. Telephone: 01877-330385. 3 rooms, all ensuite. Stone-built gamekeepers' cottage located by the riverside. Friendly, relaxed atmosphere. Great area for walking, cycling, and other outdoor activities.

Killearn, *Black Bull Hotel,* 2 The Square. Telephone: 01360-550215. Fax: 01360-550143. E-mail: blbulluk@aol.com. 10 rooms, all ensuite. Beautifully appointed nineteenth-century hotel with striking exterior: neat white trim against mustard with hanging flower baskets.

Features two restaurants, a resident's lounge, piano bar, lounge bar, and gardens.

Lochearnhead, *Mansewood Country House.* Telephone: 01567-830213. 6 rooms, all ensuite. Lovely 250-year-old manse surrounded by gardens. Features log fires, charming rooms, and warm atmosphere. Excellent restaurant also on the premises.

Perth, *Achnacarry Guest House,* Eileen and John Cowan, 3 Pitcullen Crescent. Telephone: 01738-621421. Fax: 01738-444110. 4 rooms, all ensuite. Although many guesthouses line this street, Achnacarry is one of the nicest and most welcoming ones.

Stirling, *Carol Cameron,* 10 Gladstone Place. Telephone: 01786-472681. 3 rooms, all ensuite. Handsome Victorian house, fully modernized, located in quiet residential area of town yet close to the city center and Stirling Castle.

Stirling, *Forth Guest House,* Sheena and Jim Loudon, 23 Forth Place, Riverside. Telephone: 01786-471020. Fax: 01786-447220. 6 rooms, all ensuite. Known for its hanging flower baskets and other delightful touches of color, the Forth boasts a small garden in front and compact but comfortable bedrooms. A short walk from the town center.

Strathyre, *Tony and Christine Ffinch,* Dochfour. Telephone/Fax: 01877-384256. 3 rooms, 2 ensuite. Very charming and cozy Victorian home located in the tiny village of Strathyre. Tony and Christine specialize in home cooking.

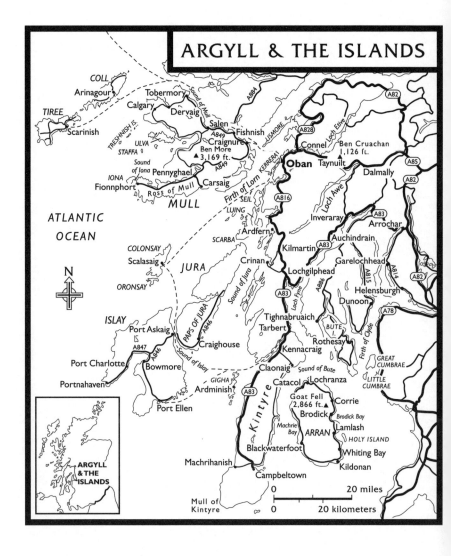

ARGYLL & THE ISLANDS

COLL
Arinagour
TIREE
Scarinish

TRESHNISH IS.
Tobermory
Calgary
Dervaig
Salen
Fishnish
ULVA
STAFFA
Craignure
Ben More
▲ 3,169 ft.
Sound
of Iona Pennyghael
IONA
Fionnphort
Ross of Mull Carsaig
MULL

Sound of Mull
A884
LISMORE
A828
Loch Etive
Connel
Ben Cruachan
1,126 ft.
Oban Taynuilt
Dalmally
KERRERA
Firth of Lorn
SEIL
LUING
A816
A849

ATLANTIC
OCEAN

N

COLONSAY
Scalasaig
ORONSAY

SCARBA
Ardfern
Inveraray
Auchindrain
Kilmartin
Crinan
Lochgilphead
JURA
Sound of Jura
PAPS OF JURA

ISLAY
Port Askaig
A847
A846
Port Charlotte
Portnahaven
Bowmore
Port Ellen

Craighouse

Sound of Islay
GIGHA
Ardminish

Claonaig
Catacol
Lochranza
Goat Fell
2,866 ft.▲
Brodick
Machrihanish
Campbeltown
Blackwaterfoot
ARRAN
Mull of
Kintyre

Kintyre

A816

Loch Awe

A83
Arrochar

Garelochhead
A815
A814
A82
Helensburgh
Dunoon
A78

Tighnabruaich
Tarbert
BUTE
I.
Rothesay
Kennacraig

Sound of Bute
GREAT
CUMBRAE
LITTLE
CUMBRAE

Corrie
Brodick Bay
Lamlash
HOLY ISLAND
Whiting Bay
Kildonan

A82
A85
A82

Loch Fyne
Firth of Clyde

0   20 miles

0   20 kilometers

ARGYLL
& THE
ISLANDS

Argyll and the Islands

It's often been said that Argyll is where the Highlands meets the Lowlands. For here two distinctive worlds—Lowland bustle and Highland grandeur—come together.

The gateway to the Hebrides is the popular ferry port and resort town of Oban. The town's most famous landmark, which is at its most impressive when viewed from the harbor, is the unfinished McCaig's Tower, or McCaig's Folly, as it is often called. Located on a hill overlooking Oban Bay, it was built by a Mr. McCaig, a local banker with apparently grandiose visions, who seemed determined to bring a piece of the Roman Colosseum to western Scotland. Alas, he died before the ambitious project was completed.

Oban has a festive nightlife in the form of eateries, lively pubs, and Scottish *ceilidhs* (parties), especially at venues like McTavish's Kitchen, a restaurant by day and club by night. Its Scottish Show continues to pack them in with its combustible combination of daft charm and contagious good spirits. The Gathering Restaurant and Ceilidh Bar on Breadalbane Street is one of the oldest restaurants in Oban. Built in 1882, it specializes in local seafood, Scottish beef, and local game. O'Donnell's Irish Pub, downstairs from the restaurant, features Celtic music and dancing most evenings.

Away from the mainland are several islands that represent the best of Scotland in miniature. The Isle of Arran, one of the Firth of Clyde islands, has been a popular destination for people trying to escape from the daily routine since the nineteenth century. Its sharply defined mountain peaks in the north and rolling hills in the south, combined with charming villages and lovely glens, have helped make Arran a perennial summer favorite for both visitors and natives. The distinctive outline of Goat Fell, at 2,866 feet the highest mountain on the island, may not be tall by world standards, but here it remains the island's best-known natural landmark.

Brodick is the largest settlement on Arran. The Isle of Arran

Heritage Museum, on the outskirts of town, is worth a visit, with its exhibits on island life from the earliest times to the 1920s. Located in Scotland's first and only island country park, the red sandstone Brodick Castle dominates an expansive area that includes a 65-acre woodland garden and eighteenth-century walled garden. Lamlash is a pretty village overlooking Brodick Bay. From the main road extend your gaze to Holy Isle, which houses a community of Tibetan Buddhists who have established a meditation center there.

Two other important Hebridean islands worth closer inspection include Mull and Iona. Tobermory, the biggest town on Mull, is a lovely and peaceful village where small gaily painted houses hug the harbor. It boasts a fine local history museum, several excellent restaurants, and even its own distillery, and is a good base for exploring the rest of the island.

In the north of the island the pretty little village of Dervaig plays host to reportedly the smallest professional theater in the United Kingdom, the Mull Little Theatre, and it contains 43 seats as proof. While here, take a few minutes to stop by the local museum, the Old Byre Heritage Centre.

Iona has been called the cradle of Scottish Christianity—quite a reputation to maintain for such a tiny island (it's only one mile wide and three and one half miles long, with a permanent population of about 100). And yet Iona looms large in the popular imagination of many a spiritual traveler. For it was here that the Irish scholar-soldier-saint Columba arrived from Ireland in 563 with a dozen disciples to establish a monastery. Fast forward to 1979, when the island was sold to the Fraser Foundation, which then committed a most charitable act—presenting it to the people of Scotland as a gift. Ultimately ownership was transferred to the National Trust for Scotland. Today it remains a popular destination for spiritual and secular traveler alike.

Most visitors stay for only a few hours before catching the ferry back to Mull—a big mistake. To fully capture the flavor, the magic, of the island you should at least stay overnight, and preferably longer. One can spend many pleasant days just wandering around the island, sitting on the white sandy beaches and watching the waves lapping up gently against the shoreline, or simply listening to the silence. And if at all possible you should attend an ecumenical service at the Iona Abbey.

Ferry Cottage
Carole and Terry Bennetton
Ardmay
Arrochar
Telephone: 01301-702428
Fax: 01301-702699
Bedrooms: 3 rooms, all ensuite.
Rates: £20-23.50 single. **Credit cards:** VISA, Eurocard, MasterCard, American Express. **Open:** January-November. **Children:** Yes, but none under 2. **Pets:** No. **Smoking:** No. **Provision for handicapped:** No. **Directions:** 1 mile south of Arrochar on the A814.

The Ferry Cottage has a nice piece of history attached to it. Originally it was the ferryman's cottage where the ferry used to run passengers across Loch Long until about 100 years ago. Today the 200-year-old cottage has been completely renovated and is now the Bennetton family home. All rooms have elevated views overlooking the loch. Despite its seemingly remote location—it really isn't that remote—the cottage is a good base for walking and hill-climbing the Arrochar Alps. Best of all, it's only a five-minute drive from the legendary braes of Loch Lomond. And after a long day's journey trudging the hills and dales, it's reassuring to know that a hearty dinner awaits you. Top off the evening with a restful sleep in your very own waterbed.

Allandale House
Valerie Somerville
Brodick
Isle of Arran
Telephone: 01770-302278
Bedrooms: 6 rooms; 5 ensuite, 1 with private shower.
Rates: £25 single. **Credit cards:** VISA, MasterCard. **Open:** January 15-
October 31. **Children:** Yes. **Pets:** Yes. **Smoking:** Restricted. **Provision for
handicapped:** Yes. **Directions:** Located a short drive from Brodick's pier.

Close to the ferry terminal, this warm and friendly B&B offers personal attention and good food. The resident's lounge, with its pinkish walls and comfortable furniture, stocks books and magazines and
is a relaxing place to enjoy a pre- or after-dinner drink. The immaculately clean rooms are attractively and cheerfully decorated. But the
secret to the success of Allandale rests with Valerie herself. She per-
forms little miracles every day. Always the gracious host, she warmly
and gently prods guests to get to know one another, so that by the time
you're finished with dinner, you will no longer remain strangers.
Indeed, as soon as you walk through the door, Valerie makes you feel
at home.

Iona Cottage
Joyce McIntyre
Isle of Iona
Telephone/Fax: 01681-700579
Bedrooms: 3 rooms, all with shared bath.
Rates: £18-25 single. **Credit cards:** None. **Open:** Year-round except Christmas and New Year's. **Children:** Yes. **Pets:** Well-behaved dogs permitted. **Smoking:** No. **Provision for handicapped:** No. **Directions:** The ferry from Oban to the Isle of Mull takes about 40 minutes. It takes about one hour to drive through Mull (there is also regular bus service available), and then a 10-minute ferry ride to Iona (no cars are allowed on the island). The cottage is about 100 yards from the ferry terminal.

This family-run B&B is housed in a charming 200-year-old cottage, just steps away from the lovely beach. The cottage is only a 10-minute walk from the Iona Abbey, the spiritual center of the island. What's more, it's also very convenient to the ferry terminal, standing as it does on a shallow rise facing the jetty. In the 1840s the cottage functioned as the island's original pub (a photograph of it in its earlier incarnation is on display in the local history museum). Its three rooms face the sea while an open fire warms visitors in the cozy sitting room. Relax and unwind amid its beautifully restored interior. Dinners typically consist of three courses followed by tea or coffee. During mealtimes guests share their meals in the sun lounge, which overlooks the Sound of Iona. All in all, it's a charming and peaceful kind of place— the kind of place you would expect to find on this most sacred of isles. Bicycle rentals can be arranged. For those on a healthy diet, please note that Joyce specializes in vegetarian cooking.

Balmoral Hotel
Jim and Linda Battison
4 Craigard Road
Oban
Telephone: 01631-562731
Fax: 01631-566810
E-mail: balmoral@oban.org.
Bedrooms: 13 rooms, 9 ensuite.
Rates: £28-33 double. **Credit cards:** Yes. **Open:** March-January.
Children: Yes. **Pets:** By arrangement. **Smoking:** Yes. **Provision for handicapped:** No. **Directions:** Located near Oban's pier, just off the town's main thoroughfare, George Street.

The Balmoral is efficiently run by the Battison family, Jim and Linda, who also happen to wear many hats. They not only run a first-rate lodging but also operate a popular and excellent seafood and steak restaurant on the first floor, one that has earned an enviable reputation for its locally caught seafood and traditional Scottish cuisine. In addition, they carry a very nice selection of fine wines and single malt whiskies. The ambiance throughout is informal and casual, the staff friendly and helpful. Balmoral is located near the pier and Oban's major attractions, yet is discreetly tucked away on a quiet side street far enough away from the noise—and being a port town, make no mistake about it, Oban can get quite rowdy at times—that it's safe to say that it offers the best of both worlds. Balmoral is a popular place in season—make sure you book in advance.

Glenbervie Guest House
Iain and Joan Auld
Dalriach Road
Oban
Telephone: 01631-564770
Fax: 01631-566723
Bedrooms: 7 rooms, 5 ensuite.
Rate: £18-25 double. **Credit cards:** No. **Open:** All year. **Children:** Yes.
Pets: No. **Smoking:** No. **Provision for handicapped:** No. **Directions:**
From George Street take Dunollie Road to Dalriach Road.

Glenbervie boasts a great location. Perched high above Oban, it offers outstanding views of the surrounding landscape, a marvelous vista of mountains, sea, and open sky. It also happens to be one of the cleanest and most comfortable B&Bs I've had the pleasure of visiting in recent years. The décor is bright and cheery throughout, and your hosts, Iain and Joan, quietly do their best to be more than accommodating, even when this means doing something beyond the call of duty. During a recent visit, I was bogged down by one too many bags and wished to make a two-day trip to Mull and Iona; the Aulds were kind enough to safeguard my luggage. Such nice touches add immeasurably to the B&B experience. Glenbervie is also convenient to the town center. A word of warning though: Dalriach Road is winding and steep. If you have heavy luggage or luggage without wheels, it is best to take a taxi from the rail station—it will cost you a few pounds, but it's worth it in the long run.

Failte Guest House
Mairi Barlow
Main Street
Tobermory
Isle of Mull
Telephone/Fax: 01688-302495
E-mail: barlow@tob302495.freeserve.co.uk
Bedrooms: 7 rooms, all ensuite.
Rates: £20 double. **Credit cards:** VISA, MasterCard. **Open:** March to October. **Children:** Yes. **Pets:** No. **Smoking:** No. **Provision for handicapped:** No. **Directions:** On the main road of town.

Failte is one of the most attractive B&Bs in town. It boasts a great location on the main road looking across Tobermory Bay. Moreover, it presents a warm beige exterior to the world that, on a bright day, almost basks in the warmth of the sun. Inside, the interior is cozy and spotlessly clean. Tobermory itself is a handsome town, with several noteworthy attractions of its own. A short walk along the main street at the southern end of the harbor will bring you to the Tobermory Distillery (there's a visitor's center and shop), while in the opposite direction lies a small but fascinating local history museum. I find that knowing something about the history of the place where I'm staying adds considerably to my visit, and since Mull has such a long and complex past, it comes highly recommended. If history is not your cup of tea, not to worry. There are two nine-hole golf courses on the island, one at Craignure and the other in Tobermory itself.

Highland Cottage
Dave and Jo Currie
Breadalbane Street
Tobermory
Isle of Mull
Telephone: 01688-302030
Fax: 01688-302727
Bedrooms: 6 rooms, all ensuite, including 2 with 4-poster beds.
Rates: £29.50-45 double. **Credit cards:** VISA, MasterCard. **Open:** Year-round **Children:** Yes. **Pets:** Well-behaved pets only. **Smoking:** Sun lounge and sitting room only. **Provision for handicapped:** Yes.
Directions: When you reach Tobermory from the Craignure or Fishnish ferries at the roundabout, take the road straight ahead crossing the narrow stone bridge. Take the first turning right and follow the road round until it opens out. Highland Cottage is the building on the right, opposite the fire station.

Dave Currie, a former training director with Sheraton Hotels in Europe, and his wife Josephine ran a successful hotel near Windsor Castle for 16 years. But they wanted something more, and their eyes looked northward, across the border. So together they conceived and built Highland Cottage—a spanking-new building set to traditional cottage design. It opened in April 1998 in a quiet area of Upper Tobermory's historic district. This is a first-rate place from top to bottom; your own home away from home. Beautifully and tastefully decorated, each room is named and given a theme after a different Scottish island. Most bedrooms come furnished with antique or four-poster beds. The fresh local ingredients are imaginatively cooked and presented. Dinner consists of four courses with coffee for £21.50. A typical meal begins with a melon accompanied by homemade pear sorbet or venison followed by Tobermory smoked salmon and trout roulade. Then take your pick of cream of carrot, tomato, or coriander soup. The main entrée is a delightful feast: roast stuffed breast of chicken or perhaps local scallops with ginger cream. To conclude try the poached pear with homemade cinnamon ice cream. There's also an extensive collection of books available for browsing on those rainy nights when nursing a Tobermory single malt seems like the right thing to do. All in all, this is a wonderful place to recharge your batteries.

ALSO RECOMMENDED

Arden, *Auchenheglish Lodge,* Mr. G. Wylie, Lomond Castle. Telephone/Fax: 01389-850688. 3 rooms, 2 ensuite. Includes a private beach and slipway on Loch Lomond. Boat rental available.

Balloch, *Station Cottages,* Marie and Eamonn McAteer, Balloch Road. Telephone: 01389-750759. Fax: 01389-710501. 2 rooms, both ensuite. Former Victorian station cottages minutes away from Loch Lomond, hotels, and restaurants.

Ballygrant, *Kilmeny Farmhouse,* Margaret Rozga, Isle of Islay. Telephone/Fax: 01496-840668. Web site: www.isleofslay.com/group/guest/kilmeny. 3 rooms, all ensuite. Attractive whitewashed farmhouse with a fine reputation for excellent food and service.

Brodick, *Dunvegan House,* Isle of Arran, David and Naomi Spencer, Shore Road. Telephone: 01770-302811. Ideally located on Brodick's seafront. David and Naomi take a personal interest in ensuring their guests are made comfortable. An excellent dinner is offered in the evenings.

Dervaig, *Cuin Lodge,* David and Dorothy Aitken. Telephone: 01688-400346. 4 rooms, 2 ensuite. Traditional nineteenth-century shooting lodge located one mile from the village of Dervaig.

Glencoe, *Clachaig Inn,* Guy and Edward Daynes. Telephone: 01855-811252. Fax: 01855-811679. E-mail: in@glencoe-scotland.co.uk. Web site: www.glencoe-scotland.co.uk. 19 rooms, most ensuite. Old drover's inn in historic Glencoe. Informal and rustic atmosphere; houses two large bars, the public bar to the rear and the lounge bar in the front, which offers spectacular views of Aonach Dubh, Glencoe's foreboding peak. Over 100 single malt whiskies are on tap. Self-catering chalets are also available.

Isle of Iona, *Argyll Hotel,* Fiona and Gordon Menzies, Isle of Iona. Telephone: 01681-700334. Fax: 01681-700510. 17 rooms; 15 ensuite and 2 singles with shared bath. Comfortable and simple converted croft house located near Iona Abbey. Savor the cozy lounges with open fires, elegant dining room, and greenhouse. Good reputation for using fresh local ingredients. Vegetarian and wholefood dishes are served. Gordon is a painter and pottery maker; his studio, Iona Pottery, is located behind the Iona Community Coffeehouse, and well worth a visit.

Lamlash, *Glenisle Hotel,* Fred and Liz, Isle of Arran. Telephone: 01770-600559. All rooms ensuite. Small and cheery country B&B. Tastefully decorated. The large garden and many of the rooms have sea views across Lamlash Bay toward Holy Isle. Excellent restaurant on the premises, too.

Oban, *Hawthornbank Guest House,* Colin and Isobel McLachlan, Dalriach Road. Telephone: 01631-562041. 8 rooms, 7 ensuite. Victorian villa overlooking Oban Bay. Features 4-poster and brass beds.

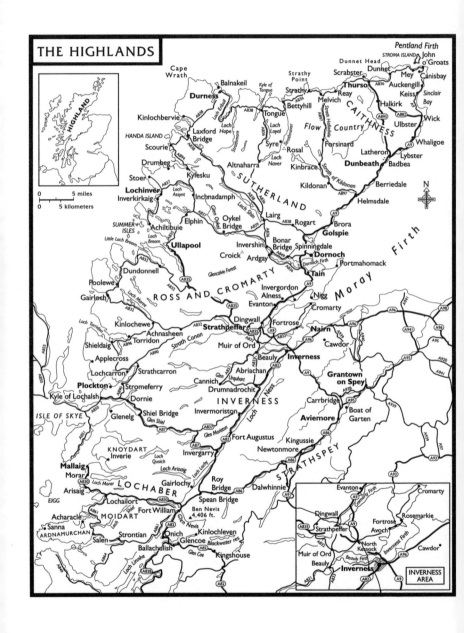

THE HIGHLANDS

HIGHLAND

Pentland Firth

STROMA ISLAND

John o'Groats

Cape Wrath

Balnakeil

Dunnet Head

Scrabster   Dunnet   Mey   Canisbay

Durness   Kyle of Tongue   Strathy Point   Strathy   Reay   Thurso   Auckengill   Keiss   Sinclair Bay

Kinlochbervie   Loch Eriboll   Tongue   Bettyhill   Melvich   Halkirk   Ulbster   Wick

HANDA ISLAND   Laxford Bridge   Loch Hope   Loch Loyal   Flow   Country   CAITHNESS   Whaligoe

Scourie   Syre   Forsinard   Latheron   Lybster   Badbea

Drumbeg   Kylesku   Altnaharra   Rosal   Kinbrace   **Dunbeath**   Berriedale

Stoer   Loch Assynt   Loch Naver   SUTHERLAND   Kildonan   Strath of Kildonan   Helmsdale

Lochinver   Inchnadamph   Lairg   Rogart   Brora

Inverkirkaig   Elphin   Oykel Bridge   Loch Shin   **Golspie**

SUMMER ISLES   Achiltibuie   Loch Broom   Invershin   Bonar Bridge   Spinningdale   **Dornoch**

Little Loch Broom   **Ullapool**   Croick   Ardgay   Dornoch Firth   Portmahomack

Dundonnell   Glencalvie Forest   **Tain**   Moray   Firth

Poolewe   Loch Maree   ROSS AND CROMARTY   Invergordon   Nigg   Cromarty

Gairloch   Loch Torridon   Alness   Evanton

Kinlochewe   Dingwall   Fortrose

Shieldaig   Achnasheen   Torridon   Strath Conon   **Strathpeffer**   **Nairn**

Applecross   Muir of Ord   Cawdor

Lochcarron   Strathcarron   Beauly   **Inverness**

Plockton   Stromeferry   Abriachan   Glen Urquhart   **Grantown on Spey**

Kyle of Lochalsh   Dornie   Cannich   Drumnadrochit   Carrbridge

ISLE OF SKYE   Glenelg   Shiel Bridge   Invermoriston   Loch Ness   **Aviemore**   Boat of Garten

Glen Shiel   INVERNESS

KNOYDART   Glen Moriston   Fort Augustus   Kingussie   STRATHSPEY

Mallaig   Inverie   Loch Quoich   Invergarry   Newtonmore

Morar   Loch Arisaig   Loch Lochy

Arisaig   Loch Morar   Gairlochy   Roy Bridge   Dalwhinnie

EIGG   LOCHABER   Spean Bridge

Acharacle   Lochailort   Fort William   Ben Nevis 4,406 ft.

Sanna   MOIDART   Glen Nevis   Kinlochleven

ARDNAMURCHAN   Strontian   Onich   Glencoe   Blackwater res.

Salen   Ballachulish   Glen Coe   Kingshouse

Loch Linnhe

N

INVERNESS AREA

Evanton   Cromarty Firth   Cromarty

Dingwall   Fortrose   Rosemarkie

Strathpeffer   Avoch

Muir of Ord   North Kessock   Cawdor

Beauly   Beauly Firth   Inverness Firth

Inverness

0   5 miles
0   5 kilometers

The Highlands

The Scotland that people imagine is the Scotland of the Highlands. The Scotland of ominous mountains breaking through a blanket of clouds; the Scotland of shimmering loch after shimmering loch; the Scotland of the world's romantic literature. The Scotland of the mind.

But there is quite a lot of truth to be discovered in this Scotland of the mind. The sights that you have seen in postcards, coffee table books, and Hollywood movies really do exist. And yet the Highlands is an exceedingly vast and complex land. To reduce it to a few stock shots culled from the Hollywood image factory is to do it a tremendous disservice. There are in fact many Highlands. Let's look at a few of them.

Caithness is the most northerly county in Britain. Much of the interior is decidedly flat. The biggest towns in this northern land are Wick and Thurso, whose names reflect their Scandinavian origins.

Ben Nevis, Britain's tallest mountain, is located in wild Lochaber, as is gorgeous Glen Nevis, considered by some to be the most beautiful glen in Scotland. It certainly appealed to the Hollywood set, since both *Braveheart* and *Rob Roy* were partially shot here.

Inverness is the largest city in the Highlands—actually the *only* city in the Highlands. With a population of approximately 60,000 for the greater "metro" area, Inverness earns its accolade as the capital of the Highlands by dint of population alone. And as expected in a capital city, it boasts a thriving cultural scene, from the Balnain House of Highland Music to Eden Court Theatre.

Further north, beyond Inverness, lies Sutherland, the least densely populated area in Europe, which stretches across much of the broad expanse of northern Scotland. Here you will find, especially in the remote northwest, the Highlands of legend. It is a brooding landscape, empty, forlorn in parts, so bleakly beautiful that it leaves you wide-eyed and speechless. It is a swirling combination of foreboding mountains, lochs, and low-lying clouds.

The Old Library Lodge & Restaurant
Angela and Alan Broadhurst
Main Road
Arisaig
Telephone: 01687-450651
Fax: 01687-450219
Bedrooms: 6 rooms, all ensuite.
Rates: £62 double. **Credit cards:** VISA, Delta, MasterCard, JCB, Eurocard, Switch. **Open:** Easter to late October. **Children:** Yes. **Pets:** No. **Smoking:** No. **Provision for handicapped:** No. **Directions:** Located along the main road of the village of Arisaig.

Arisaig offers one of the finest meals and accommodations in this part of the Highlands—hands-down. Located in the center of the tiny village of Arisaig, smack on the waterfront, it is run with great aplomb by Angela and Alan Broadhurst, who came up north from Nottingham some 15 or so years ago. Their small traditional-style restaurant is a gem to look at, light and airy, with pinkish walls. From its windows you can enjoy, in good weather, excellent views over to the Small Isles, especially the unusual rock formation known as An Sgurr on the Isle of Eigg (there is a private ferry service to Eigg and the other Small Isles from Arisaig during the season). The building itself is over 200 years old, a stone-built stable converted to a restaurant. The food is stunning, the service genuinely friendly. I enjoyed a lovely celery soup, followed by a tasty monkfish and scallop tartlet, and concluding with a spiced apple and raisin crumble with cream or ice cream. Coffee and mints are served as an after-dinner refreshment. The accommodation is equally impressive, especially the modern addition that consists

of a wing of terraced rooms with balconies overlooking a lovely garden. The bright and vibrant colors recall more of a Mediterranean
seafront resort than the western Highlands of Scotland. For those
interested in a bit of Highland literary history, the great Gaelic poet
Alexander MacDonald was born near here in 1698. He is buried in
an Arisaig graveyard in an unknown plot. A plaque sponsored by
Highland Regional Council and Scottish Natural Heritage provides
biographical information. As of this writing, a new museum, the Land,
Sea, and Islands Centre, is being erected along Arisaig's main road.

Craigellachie House
Eddie and Margaret Pedersen
Main Street
Carrbridge
Telephone/Fax: 01479-841641
Web site: www.carrbridge.com
Bedrooms: 7 rooms, some ensuite.
Rates: £16-19 double. **Credit cards:** None. **Open:** Closed December.
Children: Yes. **Pets:** No. **Smoking:** No. **Provision for handicapped:** No.
Directions: Carrbridge is 2 miles off the main A9 road. The guesthouse is situated on the main street through the village.

A warm and friendly Victorian house set in the center of the village, Craigellachie is individually decorated. Some rooms have ensuite facilities, but all come with wash/hand basin, tea- and coffee-making facilities, and central heating. Relax in the informal and comfortable resident's lounge and dining room, complete with log fires. The varied menu makes the best of local Scottish produce as well as herbs taken from their own garden. Attractions in the area are varied: golfing and fishing on the River Spey are two activities, as well as birdwatching and pony-trekking. There are also many distilleries in the area. Since Craigellachie is located in the heart of the Cairngorms, skiing is a popular pastime in the winter. Walkers and cyclists are warmly welcomed too.

Inistore Guest House
Michael and Kerensa Carr
Castle Street
Dornoch
Sutherland
Telephone: 01862-811263
Bedrooms: 2 rooms; 1 ensuite, 1 with private facilities.
Rates: £25-40 double (ensuite shower); £25-40 double/twin (private bath and shower). **Credit cards:** No. **Open:** All year. **Children:** No children under 10. **Pets:** No. **Smoking:** In lounge only. **Provision for handicapped:** No. **Directions:** Just off the A9 north of Inverness, along Dornoch's main street.

This B&B is a real find. Who would have thought that such a sophisticated restaurant and lovely accommodations could be found on the main road in this quiet northern Highland village? Yet here it is, a traditional Highland townhouse with a cozy lounge, where you can either listen to music or read books. Many people stumble across it—and what a pleasant surprise they have in store for them. Just glancing at the three-course dinner menu of the 2 Quail Restaurant (07000-2QUAIL or 01862-811811) is enough to make your mouth water: seared hot smoked salmon with guacamole and a hollandaise sauce, duck and pistachio terrine with a lime dressing, cheese and chive soufflé with red onions, and roast leg of lamb with roasted spring vegetables. And for dessert, a caramelized lemon tart with coconut ice cream. The menu changes weekly, so you'll never be sure exactly what you're going to get. Be assured that whatever is offered it will be memorable. The tasteful décor adds to the soothing and civilized atmosphere. Tables are spread out among two tartan-clad dining rooms surrounded by book-lined shelves and warm yellowish wallpaper. (The restaurant is open from Tuesday to Saturday for dinner, from 7:30-9:30 P.M.) Upstairs are several comfortable bedrooms, tastefully decorated, and surrounded by natural-grain wood. The Carrs, newcomers to the area from the north of England, opened Inistore in 1998. Michael is the chef; Kerensa personally reviews and updates the wine list (consisting primarily of French and New World wines). This B&B is a real winner over all.

Trevose Guest House
Jean Mackenzie
The Square
Dornoch
Sutherland
Telephone: 01862-810269
Bedrooms: 5 rooms, 2 ensuite.
Rates: £35 **Credit cards:** No. **Open:** March to mid-October. **Children:** Yes. **Pets:** Dogs welcome. **Smoking:** Lounge only. **Provision for handicapped:** No. **Directions:** Trevose is located directly across the street from Dornoch Cathedral, in the center of town.

Trevose is a perfectly pleasant B&B, ideally located in the center of town. Indeed, you really couldn't ask for a more ideal setting. It overlooks the village green and is across the street from lovely Dornoch Cathedral. Do have a peek inside. It's small but impressive. One particular stained-glass window has special appeal in this part of Scotland, dedicated as it is in "loving memory of A. Carnegie of Skibo 1835-1919." The wealthy Scottish-American Andrew Carnegie lived in nearby Skibo Castle for many years. (Nowadays the castle houses the Carnegie Club, a private residential golf and sporting club with an international membership limited by invitation.) Trevose itself is an attractive sandstone building, dating back to 1830. When you first arrive, and if it is a nice day, you will probably see Jean Mackenzie puttering around in the garden. The garden is a lovely one, too, full of wonderful splashes of color. Jean herself is a handsome and reserved woman but very kindhearted. Dornoch has a number of nearby attractions. The famous Royal Dornoch golf course is just a five-minute walk away. Also within the vicinity are salmon and trout fishing, as well as game shooting and pony-trekking. There are many opportunities to enjoy invigorating coastal walks and fine sandy beaches. Indeed, Dornoch boasts some of the finest beaches in Scotland. Because of its northern latitude though, you won't find too many people dipping into the water!

Dunnet Head Tearoom B&B
John and Lynette Eden
Brough Village
Dunnet Head
Near Thurso
Caithness
Telephone/Fax: 01847-851774
E-mail: bandb.farnorth@btinternet.com
Web site: www.btinternet.com/~bandb.farnorth/
Bedrooms: 3 rooms, 1 ensuite.
Rates: £15.50-18.50 p.p. **Credit cards:** None. **Open:** Easter until
September and by arrangement. **Children:** Only well-behaved chil-
dren. **Pets:** No. **Smoking:** No. **Provision for handicapped:** No.
Directions: Follow the A836 north coastal road. Turn onto the B855
road to Dunnet Head. Follow the B855 until you see the red phone
box on your right.

Dunnet Head Tearoom bears the distinction of being in the northernmost point of the Scottish mainland. Indeed, the Edens claim that
Dunnet Head is Scotland's northernmost B&B. Their cozy house
offers views across the sea over twin rock stacks to Orkney. Seals bask
on the rocks and, if you're lucky, you'll be able to see otters frolicking during twilight hours. (During summer months it never gets truly
dark up here.) Bird life is also abundant. The tearoom was originally
an old inn: sailing ships used to carry grain from Caithness onto such
far-away destinations as Canada and Scandinavia. The Edens have a
ham radio station for visitors to try their hand at. And, if you need to
keep in touch with the outside world, you can also send E-mail from

here. Horses are kept in the rear in two stables. The Edens are knowl-
edgeable about travel throughout the United Kingdom and can easily arrange day trips to Orkney for about £30 per person, which
includes tour and sea crossing. John is an ex-RAF member with a background in industrial electronics and small businesses. Lyn's family
business was in catering. Small and unpretentious, Dunnet Head wel-
comes unpretentious people. The Edens truly care about their guests
and their well-being; they treat people as they would like to be treated
themselves.

Daviot Mains Farm
Margaret and Alex Hutcheson
Daviot
Near Inverness
Telephone: 01463-772215
Fax: 01463-772099
E-mail: farmhols@globalet.co.uk
Bedrooms: 3 rooms, 2 ensuite.
Rates: £24 double twin ensuite. Single room supplement of £7 from May 1 to September 30. **Credit cards:** MasterCard, VISA. **Open:** Year-round except Christmas Eve and Christmas Day. **Children:** Yes; discounts for children under 12 sharing room with two adults. **Pets:** Dogs by arrangement. **Smoking:** No. **Provision for handicapped:** No.
Directions: Located on the B851 road just off the main A9, about 6 miles south of Inverness. Take the B851 to Croy. The farm is .75 mile further along.

Daviot is an early nineteenth-century farmhouse located in a quiet area near Inverness. It offers an unusual design: four wings enclose a central courtyard. The immaculately clean bedrooms are all named after nearby rivers. The Hutchesons have been entertaining guests for almost 20 years now, and their enthusiasm shows no signs of abating. Indeed, they have made many lasting friendships over the years, especially among Americans, "and now," says Margaret, "have a lengthy Christmas card list over the water." Homemade goodies—scones and shortbread—are offered as a "nightcap." Dinner is also quite special here. Traditional Scottish dishes that may appear on your plate include fresh locally caught salmon and trout, meats, vegetables, cheeses, and seasonal fruits. Enjoy the comfy sitting room in front of the log fire.

The Osprey Hotel
Robert and Aileen Burrow
Ruthven Road
Kingussie
Telephone/Fax: 01540-661510
E-mail: aileen@ospreyhotel.freeserve.co.uk
Web site: www.ospreyhotel.freeserve.co.uk
Bedrooms: 8 rooms; 6 ensuite and 2 private.
Rates: £22-30; £39-49 with dinner. **Credit cards:** MasterCard/Eurocard, American Express, VISA, Diners Club. **Open:** All year. **Children:** Yes. **Pets:** No. **Smoking:** Restricted. **Provision for handicapped:** No. **Directions:** Located on the southern portion of Kingussie, just off the main A9 trunk road; about 300 meters from the main Inverness to London main station.

The Osprey is a small hotel overlooking the Memorial Gardens in the center of the Highland village of Kingussie. Informal yet elegant, the personal touch of owners Robert and Aileen is evident everywhere, from the tasteful décor to the elegant meals. Red-carpeted hallways make for a truly warm welcome. The eight pretty rooms are quiet and cozy and come with private facilities, color television, clock radio/alarm, refreshment tray, electric blanket, and hair dryer. After dinner, relax in one of their two lounges and choose from a nicely chosen selection of malt whisky, port, brandy, or liqueur. Evening meals are among the best in town. Specialties include prime beef, venison, game, salmon, and trout. All are imaginatively presented with a certain flair: pecan and apple soup with a hint of curry for starters, salmon with leek and tarragon as the entrée, and for dessert chocolate and orange roulade followed by coffee and mints. The Burrows also offer an excellent selection of European country wines as well as wines from Australia, New Zealand, North and South America, and South Africa. The breakfast menu typically consists of porridge, oak-smoked haddock and kippers, local heather honey, and freshly ground coffee. The breads and rolls are baked daily in their own kitchen.

Sonnhalde
Janis and Bernie Jones
East Terrace
Kingussie
Telephone: 01540-661266
Bedrooms: 7 rooms, 3 ensuite.
Rates: From £18 per person; dinner and B&B from £27. **Credit cards:** No. **Open:** Year-round. **Children:** Yes. **Pets:** No. **Smoking:** In lounge only. **Provision for handicapped:** Yes. **Directions:** Approaching the village traffic lights from the south, turn left. Then make a right turn into East terrace. Sonnhalde is the third house on the left.

Bernie Jones is full of rambunctious energy and he's a keen photographer to boot (he also runs a photo studio called B+J Photography). Bernie and his wife Janis run this spic-and-span B&B, which is located up a steep incline, with wonderful views across the Spey Valley to the Ruthven Barracks ruins and the Cairngorm mountains beyond. The name means "Sunnybank"—it's located on a bank, sometimes sunny, sometimes not, just above High Street beside the town clock. The rooms in this 100-year-old building are spacious and comfortable, the décor warm. The hanging plants reflect Bernie's love of nature. He is also an avid birdwatcher, and this energetic Yorkshireman is glad to offer nature and photographic tours (including field trips and darkroom and studio use) to the area's glens and surrounding countryside. While in town you must stop by the excellent Highland Folk Museum on Duke Street. The highlight of the museum's collections is most certainly the Isle of Lewis Blackhouse, a replica of a traditional thatched

Highland dwelling. For a relaxing bite to eat, check out Gilly's Kitchen along High Street, which offers a surprisingly sophisticated menu for a small café: Rannoch smoked venison paté with toast, couscous potato salad, or baguettes and croissants with roasted vegetables in olive oil.

Culduthel Lodge
David and Marion Bonsor
14 Culduthel Road
Inverness
Telephone/Fax: 01463-240089
Bedrooms: 12 rooms, all ensuite.
Rates: £80-95. **Credit cards:** VISA, MasterCard. **Open:** Year-round.
Children: 10 and older **Pets:** By arrangement. **Smoking:** Most rooms
are non-smoking. **Provision for handicapped:** No. **Directions:** Located
along Culduthel Road, a short drive off Inverness's High Street.

My vote for the best accommodations in Inverness goes to the
Culduthel. David and Marion Bonsor offer the best in Highland hospitality and graciousness. This Georgian beauty is located in an attractively upscale section of Inverness, a short walk away from the River
Ness, and set on its own grounds. The traditional drawing room has
large windows that look out over Inverness and the surrounding hills.
On arrival, guests will appreciate several small and thoughtful touches:
fresh fruit, a small decanter of sherry, and a CD/cassette/radio player.
Among the other services are 24-hour laundry service and a complimentary daily newspaper of your choice. In pleasant weather, enjoy a
glass of wine or a cup of tea on the outdoor terrace. David, your tall
and handsome host, will likely be the one serving your morning coffee
or full Scottish breakfast. Drinks and light snacks are available until
midnight in the drawing room, your bedroom, or on the terrace. A
homey fixture of Culduthel Lodge is the sight of Shelly, the family
dog, reclining lazily in all her glory in the hallway or by the door.
Culduthel may be a first-class lodge, but it still offers its down-home
touches—thank goodness.

East Dene Guest House
Phyllis and Don Greig
6 Ballifeary Road
Inverness
Telephone: 01463-232976
Fax: 01463-232976
E-mail: dgreig@nildram.co.uk
Website: www.SmoothHound.co.uk/hotels/eastd.html
Bedrooms: 4 rooms; 3 ensuite, 1 room with private bathroom.
Rates: £24-28. **Credit cards:** VISA and MasterCard. **Open:** Year-round.
Children: 12 and up. **Pets:** No. **Smoking:** Restricted. **Provision for
handicapped:** No. **Directions:** Situated on the north side of the River
Ness, close to Eden Court Theatre, between Glenurquhart Road
(A82) and the Ness Walk.

The Greig's children were brought up in this traditional stone-built
Victorian house. Their departure made the place feel cold and empty,
so Don and Phyllis, given their gregarious nature, did the most logi-
cal thing they could think of—they invited the world to stay with them.
The rooms are tastefully decorated, the lounge comfortable. East
Dene is conveniently located less than 10 minutes from the town center. Also nearby are numerous golf courses, bowling greens, tennis and
squash courts, fishing, and other leisure and recreational facilities.
St. Andrews Cathedral is also within walking distance.

Ivy Bank Guest House
Catherine Cameron
28 Old Edinburgh Road
Inverness
Telephone: 01463-232796
Fax: 01463-232796
Website: www.SmoothHound.co.uk/hotels/ivybank.html
Bedrooms: 5 rooms, 3 ensuite.
Rates: From £22.50. **Credit cards:** None. **Open:** Year-round. **Children:** Yes. **Pets:** Well-behaved dogs. **Smoking:** No. **Provision for handicapped:** No. **Directions:** From the A82, continue across the bridge, up Castle Street. The guesthouse is at the top of the hill.

Built in 1836, this historic Georgian building is full of great character and charm. The interior design reeks of the warmth of another era: oak paneling, mahogany staircase, open fires, and original fireplaces. Ivy Bank is located within a five-minute walk to the town center. The tastefully decorated lounge is a wonderful place to relax, watch television, or, should the mood possess you, even play a few chords on the baby grand piano. The ensuite bedrooms have bath and shower facilities, and one ensuite room has a fourposter bed. Adding to the charm is a walled and landscaped garden and pond. Overall, Ivy Bank is an enjoyable place to unwind and savor life's little pleasures.

The Old Smiddy
Kate and Steve Macdonald
Laide
Near Gairloch
Telephone/Fax: 01445-731425
E-mail: oldsmiddy@aol.com
Website: www.s-h-systems.co.uk/hotels/oldsmid/html
Bedrooms: 3 rooms with private facilities.
Rates: £24-32. **Credit cards:** MasterCard, VISA. **Open:** April-October.
Children: Over 12. **Pets:** Yes. **Smoking:** No. **Provision for handicapped:**
No. **Directions:** From Inverness take the A835 to Braemore junction,
then turn left onto the A832. Take the road that indicates coastal
route to Gairloch, Aultbea, and Dundonnell. Go toward Little
Gruinard. Old Smiddy is the house on the left opposite the church
beside the forest.

The Old Smiddy is probably one of the most romantic lodgings
you'll find anywhere in Scotland. Maybe it has something to do with its
candlelight dinners, warm and relaxed atmosphere, and its friendly
hosts, Kate and Steve. Kate is a native of Fort William and a former
nurse. On arrival guests are greeted with a complimentary tray of tea
or coffee and home-baked goodies. Each room comes with complimentary mineral water, chocolates, toiletries, electric blankets, radio
alarms, and shoe and sewing kits. There is also a 24-hour laundry service for a small fee. In addition, the MacDonalds can arrange fishing
permits on a daily or weekly basis. Eventually preparations for the
evening meal will be discussed. The choices are plentiful, from filo
baskets stuffed with west coast mussels and bacon in a lemon and wine

sauce to homemade red and yellow pepper soup with sesame toast. And that's just the starters. For your main dish you may be offered roast wild salmon on a bed of spiced cabbage leaves or perhaps a leg of lamb soaked in a red wine and wild mushroom sauce. Desserts may consist of pear and almond torte with fresh cream or yogurt or perhaps something simpler, such as homemade ice cream and fruit. End the meal with coffee or tea accompanied with a piece of homemade fudge. Breakfast here is a major feast, too. It starts with a choice of fresh fruit juices, cereals or muesli, and yogurt with fresh fruit or compote of fruit. Try the porridge made with stone-ground Golspie oatmeal from the last remaining water-driven mill in Scotland. And then the real breakfast begins: sausage, black pudding, bacon, free-range eggs, mushrooms, tomatoes, and fried bread or scrambled eggs with smoked salmon served on hot buttered toast and topped with grilled tomatoes. Or how about grilled Scottish cheddar cheese on white or brown toast? You will probably also be offered traditional and herbal teas, a jug of coffee, or hot chocolate, not to mention the various homemade breads, scones, and oatcakes.

Jean Crocket
Jean Crocket
1 Loch Nevis Crescent
Mallaig
Telephone: 01687-462171
Bedrooms: 2 rooms with private facilities.
Rates: £16 pp. **Credit cards:** No. **Open:** April-October. **Children:** Yes.
Pets: No. **Smoking:** No. **Provision for handicapped:** No. **Directions:**
Proceed through Mallaig until you reach the fire station. Jean Crocket
is opposite the station.

Jean Crocket is a tiny wisp of a woman, and the perfect Highland
host. Not only does she make you feel an instant member of the
household, she makes sure everyone else is happy and content too.
As soon as you arrive, your quick-footed and diminutive host wastes no
time in offering you a cup of tea and biscuits in the wood-paneled
lounge. And if you happen to be traveling alone and other guests are
staying as well, she takes great pleasure in turning strangers into
acquaintances. No eating in silence while at the Crocket residence.
She and her husband Andrew, both of whom are retired, take great
pleasure in sharing their home with the rest of the world. The utterly
charming white stucco house is hard to miss: it's the one with the garden out front decorated with miniature windmills, trolls, sea otters,
and other delightful knickknacks. The rooms are exceedingly lovely
and cozy; the views across Mallaig Harbor are splendid. But most of all
it is Jean's warmth that you will most likely take away with you.

Tigh-na-Clash Guest House
Joan and Ian Ritchie
81 Melvich
By Thurso
Sutherland
Telephone/Fax: 01641-531262
Bedrooms: 3 rooms (Call to confirm).
Rates: Call to confirm. **Credit cards:** No. **Open:** April-October.
Children: Yes. **Pets:** No. **Smoking:** No smoking in bedrooms or din-
ing room. **Provision for handicapped:** No. **Directions:** Tigh-na-Clash is
the first B&B on the left heading north from Helmsdale, opposite
the Halladale Inn.

Located in the small coastal Sutherland village of Melvich in
Scotland's remote north, Tigh-Na-Clash offers modern lodging at its
finest. All rooms come with television, tea-making facilities, and the
like. What sets it apart from other accommodations is the personal
touch of the Ritchies. They do their best to make their guests feel
comfortable, as if they had just arrived home from a long journey. It
doesn't hurt either that wonderful views can be observed from the
resident's lounge. The Ritchies offer an immaculate house as well as
an attractive garden. Breakfast is a bit on the unusual side, too. In
addition to the standard items, they have also added smoked haddock and kippers to the selections. The nearest towns are Thurso and
Scrabster, where you can catch the ferry to Orkney. Also in the vicinity is John O'Groats. Although little more than a tourist trap, many
people who make the effort to venture this far north can't resist coming here, the northernmost settlement on the Scottish mainland.

Much wilder is Cape Wrath. Ask the Ritchies for the best way to get there. Alternatively, Sutherland is a nature lover's paradise. Here you are in the heart of Flow Country, a watery wilderness of peatlands, and the RSPB Reserve at Forsinard. Birdwatching and hill-walking are just some of the more popular activities up here. But, in good weather, there are also plenty of beaches to enjoy (given the temperature of the water, bathing is not recommended, though), fishing, surfing, and even diving (not for the timid). Nearby museums include the Timespan Museum in Helmsdale and the Strathnaver Museum at Bettyhill. Both have significant displays on the Highland Clearances. Again, ask the Ritchies for their seasoned advice.

The Sheiling Guest House
Joan and Hugh Campbell
Melvich
North Sutherland
By Thurso
Telephone/Fax: 01641-531256
E-mail: thesheiling@btinternet.com
Web site: www.host.co.uk
Bedrooms: 3 rooms, all ensuite.
Rates: £22-24. **Credit cards:** None. **Open:** March-November. **Children:** Yes. **Pets:** By arrangement only. **Smoking:** No. **Provision for handicapped:** No. **Directions:** Drive north on the A9. Catch the A897 at Helmsdale for 40 miles. Turn left onto the A836 coastal junction. The Sheiling is 2 miles further along.

The Sheiling serves as an excellent base to tour Caithness and Sutherland and to make that day trip across the Pentland Firth to Orkney. Your Sutherland-born hosts bring with them some 30 years of experience in the tourist industry. Their home is situated on 15 acres of hill-crofting ground. Besides the gorgeous views up this way, the real reason to stay at the Sheiling is to savor the terrific breakfasts. A buffet table includes orange and grapefruit juice, a variety of cold cereals, unusual fruit compotes (rhubarb and melon, banana and orange, fresh raspberries and strawberries), porridge, and homemade yogurt with fruit preserves. Grilled items could include wild brown trout or fresh herring dipped in oatmeal, natural oak smoked haddock with poached egg, smoked salmon, Aberdeen kippers, or French toast with peppered tomatoes. Also on hand for this bountiful feast are various breads and Scottish oatcakes with homemade jams (rhubarb, lemon curd, plum, gooseberry, black currant, strawberry, and raspberry). The Campbells have two comfy lounges: the television lounge overlooks Melvich Bay; the sitting room, which faces west and overlooks the garden, is the place to read or play board games. The Campells' motto is simple: "We are here for your pleasure . . . our home is your home."

Sunny Brae Hotel
Sylvia and Ian Bochel
Marine Road
Nairn
Telephone: 01667-452309
Fax: 01667-454860
E-mail: sunnybrae@easynet.co.uk
Web site: vacations-scotland.co.uk/sunnybrae.html
Bedrooms: 9 rooms, all ensuite.
Rates: From £35 pp. **Credit cards:** VISA and MasterCard. **Open:** March-November. **Children:** Well-behaved children only. **Pets:** By arrangement only. **Smoking:** Lounge only. **Provision for handicapped:** No, but they have five ground-floor rooms. **Directions:** From Inverness take the roundabout on the A96. Go to the first exit, and then proceed straight ahead for another 350 yards.

Nairn has been a resort town for decades, and Sylvia and Ian do their best to encourage visitors to take full advantage of the many attractions in the vicinity. From the lounge, dining room, front bed-rooms, and sun terrace, you can see lovely uninterrupted views over the Moray Firth. This completely modernized family-run hotel offers high standards of comfort, attentive service, and cuisine prepared from fresh, local, quality produce and seafood. Ian and Sylvia and their two sons John and Alexander are a handsome family. Living up to the B&B's name, the rooms are indeed sunny, and the attention that the Bochels spend on details is impressive. Each room is individually dec-orated and spotlessly clean. The color schemes are unusually pleasing to the eye (yellow pillows on blue chairs). Whenever possible, regular visitors are given their favorite rooms—a nice personal touch. There are always plenty of things to do in the area, from golfing and indulging in a boat trip or two, to some serious beachcombing. (Nairn has earned a reputation for having a mild climate—not exactly Miami Beach, mind you, but warm enough to at least be able to enjoy the sunshine.) In this neck of the woods a favorite pastime is dolphin watching. Numerous historic sites are nearby, including Cawdor Castle, Culloden Battlefield, and Fort George. Of course, Nessie is close by too.

Seabank Bed & Breakfast
Alasdair and Lynn Bruce
6 Bank Street
Plockton
Telephone: 01599-544221
Fax: 01599-544221
E-mail: abruce@btinternet.com
Bedrooms: 3, 1 ensuite.
Rates: £18-22.50, double. **Credit cards:** None. **Open:** Year-round.
Children: Yes. **Pets:** Yes. **Smoking:** Yes. **Provision for handicapped:** No.
Directions: From Plockton railway station, continue down the hill, past the primary school at the bottom on the right. Seabank is located behind the school. Parking is available behind the house or in the car park.

This small and recently restored cottage boasts a garden that faces directly onto the shore of lovely Loch Carron. Seabank is located in the historic village of Plockton, which is known for both its charm and its spectacular natural surroundings (it was voted Highland Village of the Year in 1994). The popular BBC television series *Hamish MacBeth* was filmed here. (Its star, Robert Carlyle, has since gone onto to even bigger things, including starring roles in *The Full Monty* and, most recently, *Angela's Ashes.*) Plockton is a good base for walking, boat trips, or visiting Skye (the notorious Skye Bridge is only a short six-mile drive away). Seabank itself is perfectly situated in a quiet part of the village by the water's edge and within easy walking distance of numerous hotels, shops, and restaurants. Most rooms have a view of the loch.

The Sheiling
Jane and John MacDonald
Plockton
Telephone: 01599-544282
Fax: 01599-544282
E-mail: jane@shieling282.freeserve.co.uk
Bedrooms: 3 rooms, 1 ensuite.
Rates: £18-22. **Credit cards:** None. **Open:** Easter-October. **Children:** Over age 12. **Pets:** No. **Smoking:** In lounge only. **Provision for handicapped:** Suitable for some disabled people; call for arrangements.
Directions: Drive into the village and along the harbor street. Turn right by the village hall then right again at the end of the road. The Sheiling is situated on the edge of the peninsula.

In my humble opinion, the MacDonalds are blessed with one of the finest views in Plockton. Situated on a slight peninsula, the Sheiling feels both isolated and safe. The vantage point from the town itself makes it appear very inviting—a tiny, whitewashed cottage on its own (to get here you must follow the footpath along the narrow causeway). In reality, the MacDonalds have a comfortable family home in an exceedingly picturesque historic village, with panoramic views over the loch from their spacious lounge, which in turn leads to the garden. Whichever way you look—toward the village itself or the surrounding loch—the views are mighty impressive. Plockton is an ideal base for touring the surrounding countryside. It's also a gateway to Skye, since the famed island is only a short drive away. But do spend some time in the village of Plockton itself. In recent years it has become a familiar sight to TV watchers in Britain—the popular *Hamish MacBeth* series is shot here. With its palm trees, traditional red telephone booths, and snug cottages, it is a perfect place to relax and do absolutely nothing.

Cloisters
Bob and Audrey Morrison
Church Holme
Talmine
Sutherland
Telephone/Fax: 01847-601286
Bedrooms: 3 rooms, all ensuite.
Rates: £20-25. **Credit cards:** None. **Open:** All year. **Children:** From age 12. **Pets:** Yes, if house-trained. **Smoking:** No. **Provision for handicapped:** 1 room is wheelchair accessible. **Directions:** Follow the A9 North sign, then turn off onto the B817 near Evanton to Bonar Bridge. Take the A836 from Bonar Bridge to Lairg (approximately 11 miles), and continue on the A836 to Tongue (approximately 40 miles). Leave Tongue on the A838 causeway, turn right to Melness and Talmine on unclassified road (about 3 miles). Pass through Skinnet Pass, with the Craggan Hotel on the left. Cloisters is ahead on a small road on the left. If you reach Talmine post office, you have gone too far.

As its name indicates, the Cloisters' former life was that of a nineteenth-century church. Interior archways recall this former life. Located in the village of Talmine on the Kyle of Tongue, the Cloisters offers marvelous sea views over inshore islands to Orkney beyond. The surrounding area is also studded with historic landmarks, from Bronze Age remains to Clearance villages. Your hosts have quite a fascinating background. Bob Morrison was born in Nairn and is a retired architect who spent most of his working life in Australia's Northern Territory. He plays clarinet with a local jazz group. Audrey is from Aberdeen and is a retired classical ballet teacher who also spent most of her working life in Australia, running her own ballet school in Darwin. Aberdeen-born Iain was raised in Australia and operates Highlander Photographic Safaris, a six day/five night all-inclusive package holiday that offers customized tours tailored to suit various interests, from history and archaeology to wildlife and photography (maximum: 6 passengers). Continental, vegetarian, or full Scottish breakfast is served either in the dining room or sun lounge overlooking Talmine Bay. Packed lunches can be provided upon request.

The Ceilidh Place
Jean Urquhart
14 West Argyle Street
Ullapool
Telephone: 01854-612103
Fax: 01854-612886
Bedrooms: 15 rooms in main building.
Rates: £60 pp. **Credit cards:** Yes. **Open:** Year-round. **Children:** Yes. **Pets:** By arrangement. **Smoking:** Yes. **Provision for handicapped:** No.
Directions: Located in the center of the village, just north of the harbor.

It's hard to believe that the Ceilidh Place started out in the 1970s in such a humble way—by serving light refreshments and entertainment in a former boat shed—for today it is one of the premier lodgings in all of Scotland. But more than just a hotel or B&B, the Ceilidh Place is also an excellent restaurant, casual café, pub, art gallery, bookshop, and all-around entertainment center. Light meals and snacks are served cafeteria-style in the café (vegetarian food and local seafood are specialties). The restaurant offers fine dining at its best. There is also an excellent selection of malt whiskies, wines, and ales in the pub. But what really sets the place apart is the ongoing entertainment held throughout the year: concerts, literary events, plays, exhibitions, and slide lectures. You name it, the Ceilidh Place does it, from traditional Scottish music to the Mississippi Delta blues. The main white two-story building consists of 15 rooms(8 double, 4 twin, and 3 single bed-rooms),while the college dormitory-type setting of the clubhouse offers comfort at considerably lower prices—about £15 for a single (breakfast is extra though). It's all very rustic and collegiate in the clubhouse with its bunk beds, wooden furniture, and communal facilities. Ullapool has several sites worth visiting, including the small Ullapool Bookshop and Museum and its larger counterpart the Ullapool Museum, which has a terrific exhibition on emigration from the Loch Broom area to Nova Scotia.

Summer Isles Hotel
Mark and Gerry Irvine
Achiltibuie
By Ullapool
Telephone: 01854-622282
Fax: 01854-622251
E-mail: smilehotel@aol.com
Bedrooms: 13 rooms, all with private bath.
Rates: £50-60. **Credit cards:** MasterCard/Eurocard, VISA, Switch.
Open: Easter-early October. **Children:** From 6 years. **Pets:** By arrangement. **Smoking:** Restricted. **Provision for handicapped:** No.
Directions: From Inverness take the A835 northwest to Ullapool.
Summer Isles is located 10 miles beyond Ullapool. Turn left onto a single-track road. An additional 15 miles on will bring you to the village. The hotel is 1 mile past the village entrance on the left.

Summer Isles was originally built during the mid-nineteenth century for the fishing tenants on the Cromarty estate. Since the Irvines bought it in 1969, it has become a haven of civilization in a stunning yet remote part of Scotland. The major draws around here are the Summer Isles' food and the gorgeous scenery. The tiny village of Achiltibuie consists of a line of white cottages looking over the bay toward the evocatively named Summer Isles. Although warmed by the gulf stream, Mark and Gerry are quick to stress that the weather can change suddenly, from "Arctic to Aegean inside a week," so be prepared. The scent of the sea is everywhere. So it's not surprising to learn that nearly everything on your breakfast and dinner plates is home produced or locally caught: scallops, lobsters, crabs, halibut, turbot, and salmon, as well as venison, brown eggs, and brown bread fresh from the oven. The Irvines best sum up the appeal of Summer Isles: "a marvelous amount of nothing to do." Actually there is plenty to do if you enjoy fishing, birdwatching, or walking the trails (anywhere from 3 to 30 miles). The *Hectoria* is a local cruise boat that takes people around the islands to view seals and rare species of birds. There is also a diving school nearby, or you can take the Irvines' advice and simply relax. Nothing is rushed here. About the only timetable you need to worry about is dinner. It is served promptly at 8 o'clock sharp.

ALSO RECOMMENDED

Ballachulish, *Craiglinnhe Guest House.* Telephone: 01855-811270. Elegant Victorian guesthouse overlooking Loch Linnhe. All rooms are ensuite. Excellent food and lodging at reasonable prices.

Ballachulish, *Lyn-Leven Guest House,* John and Priscilla MacLeod, West Laroch, near Fort William. Telephone: 01855-811392. Fax: 01855-811600. 8 rooms, all ensuite. This modern bungalow with a lovely garden overlooks Loch Leven. Vegetarian meals are their specialty.

Boat of Garten, *Heathbank—The Victorian House,* Lindsay and Graham Burge. Telephone: 01479-831234. 7 rooms, all ensuite. Turn-of-the-century Victorian country house set in its own gardens. Two of the rooms have 4-poster beds and are tastefully decorated with flourishes of period charm. Fresh soups, homemade breads, local game and fish, and Scottish beef and lamb are served to guests.

Cromarty, *The Retreat B&B,* Church Street. Telephone: 01381-600400. Former 18th-century merchant's house, small and neat. Cromarty is the jewel of the Black Isle, a wonderfully atmospheric town known for its vernacular Georgian-style architecture.

Culloden Moor, *King of Clubs,* Vanne P. Fraser, Tigh-na-Ceard, Sunnyside, near Inverness. Telephone/Fax: 01463-790476. E-mail: kingofclubs@mail.easynet.co.uk. 2 rooms, both ensuite. Friendly and tastefully decorated, with spacious rooms. Its name derives from their main source of business: custom golf-club makers and repairers. King of Clubs is a 10-minute walk from Culloden battlefield and a 10-minute drive to Inverness town center.

Drumnadrochit, *Drumbuie Farm,* Mrs. C. Urquhart, Loch Ness. Telephone: 01456-450634. Fax: 01456-450595. 3 rooms, all ensuite. Livestock farm; highland cattle. This working farm overlooks Loch Ness.

Fort Augustus, *Fort Augustus Abbey on Loch Ness,* Inverness-shire. Telephone: 01320-366233. Fax: 01320-366228. E-mail: abbey@monk.co.uk. Web site: www.monk.co.uk. 29 rooms. Simply furnished rooms, Spartan and clean. There is also a game room, television lounge, and "quiet" lounge in addition to a fine restaurant on the premises and a heritage center. Loch Ness cruises can be arranged.

Fort William, *Taransay House,* Mary Murray, Seafield Gardens. Telephone: 01397-703303. 3 rooms, 1 with private facilities. Modern accommodations about a 15- to 20-minute walk from the town center. Offers panoramic views overlooking Loch Linnhe. Mary Murray is your delightful host.

Inverness, *Trafford Bank,* the MacKenzie family, 96 Fairfield Road. Telephone: 01463-241414. E-mail: traff@pop.cali.co.uk. 5 rooms, all ensuite. Comfortable and spacious, this Victorian house is just a 10-minute walk from the town center in a quiet residential area. Complimentary fruit and flowers in all rooms.

Kingussie, *The Hermitage Guest House,* David and Marie Taylor, Spey Street. Telephone/Fax: 01540-662137. E-mail: thehermitage@clara.net. The Taylors offer comfortable bedrooms with ensuite facilities, a resident's lounge with log fires on cold evenings, and a large garden with views of the Cairngorm mountains.

Kyle of Lochalsh, *Retreat Guest House,* Donald and Catherine Callander, Main Street. Telephone/Fax: 01599-534090. Attractive and friendly family-run lodging on the road to Skye. Excellent restaurant on the premises. Handsomely furnished rooms, too. Seagreen Restaurant & Bookshop, a short walk from the guest house, serves excellent local seafood and wholefood dishes. Housed in the old village school, it also features exhibitions and traditional music.

Lairg, *Park House,* Ms. M. E. Walker, Station Road. Telephone: 01549-402208. Fax: 01549-402693. 3 rooms, all ensuite. Overlooking Loch Shin, the Park House offers spacious rooms and home-cooked meals. Brown trout and salmon fishing or golfing on five local golf courses can be arranged.

Plockton, *Plockton Hotel,* Dorothy and Tom Pearson, Harbour Street. Telephone: 01599-544274. Fax: 01599-544475. Web site: www.host.co.uk. 4 rooms, all ensuite. Small and friendly with lots of atmosphere. Two of the front bedrooms overlook the loch. The wonderful restaurant offers friendly service, a maritime flavor, and cozy atmosphere. Specialties include local shellfish, especially prawns, and char-grilled steaks.

Spean Bridge, *Barbagianni Guest House,* Tirindrish. Telephone: 01397-712437. 7 rooms, all ensuite. Absolutely lovely guesthouse that offers not only spectacular views of Ben Nevis and comfortable accommodations but also attentive and caring service.

Strathpeffer, *Craigvar,* Margaret S. L. Scott, The Square. Telephone: 01997-421622. Fax: 01997-421796. E-mail: m.s.@gilsmith.demon.co.uk. 3 rooms, all ensuite. Handsome Georgian house overlooking the town square in a former Victorian spa village. Many personal touches, including a fourposter bed.

Strathy Point, *Sharvedda,* P. A. MacAskill, by Thurso. Telephone: 01641-541311. 3 rooms, 2 ensuite. Small working croft with superb views to Orkney and Dunnet Head. Popular with hill-walkers and bird-watchers. The large spacious lounge has an open peat fire in the winter. The dinner menu emphasizes traditional locally made foods. Home baking is a specialty.

By Thurso, *Aultivullin,* Donald and Margaret MacKay, Strathy Point. Telephone: 01641-541235. 3 rooms. Traditional crofthouse, immaculately and lovingly kept. Among the attractions in the area are a sandy beach at Strathy Bay and grassy dunes.

Ullapool, *Brae Guest House,* Shore Street. Telephone: 01854-612421. 11 rooms, 10 ensuite. Pretty, clean, and cozy. Cruises, sailing, and water-skiing on Loch Broom can be arranged.

Ullapool, *The Sheiling Guest House,* Duncan and Mhairy MacKenzie, Garve Road. Telephone: 01854-612947. 7 rooms, all ensuite. Situated above the main road to Ullapool, the Sheiling offers panoramic views of lovely Loch Broom. Cheery bedrooms. The lounge and dining room overlook the loch.

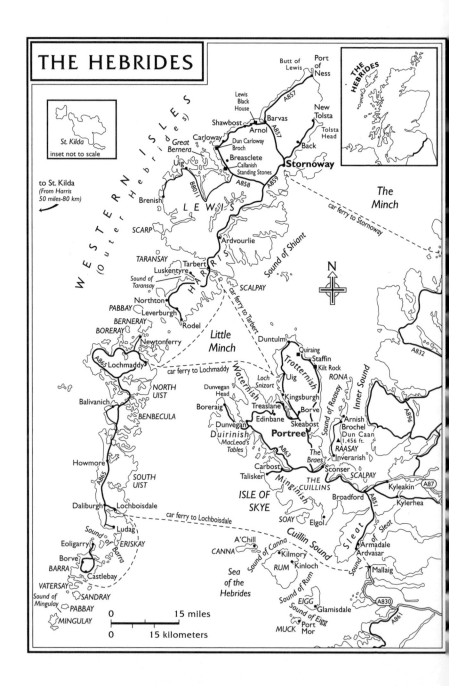

THE HEBRIDES

St. Kilda
inset not to scale

to St. Kilda
(From Harris
50 miles-80 km)

WESTERN ISLES
(Outer Hebrides)

Butt of
Lewis
Port
of
Ness

Lewis
Black
House

New
Tolsta

Shawbost
Barvas
A857
A857

Carloway
Tolsta
Head

Dun Carloway
Broch
Back

Great
Bernera

Breasclete
Callanish
Standing Stones

Stornoway

Uig

A858

A857

B8011

Brenish

L E W I S

car ferry to Stornoway

The
Minch

SCARP

Ardvourlie

Sound of Shiant

TARANSAY

Tarbert
Luskentyre

Sound of
Taransay

H A R R I S

SCALPAY

N

Northton
Leverburgh

PABBAY

BERNERAY

BORERAY

Rodel

Little
Minch

Duntulm

car ferry to Tarbert

Newtonferry

Quiraing
Staffin
Kilt Rock

A832

A865
Lochmaddy

car ferry to Lochmaddy

Trotternish

Waternish

Loch
Snizort

Uig

RONA

NORTH
UIST

Dunvegan
Head

Kingsburgh

Sound of Raasay

Inner Sound

Balivanich

Boreraig

Treaslane
Edinbane

Borve

BENBECULA

Dunvegan

Skeabost

Portree

Arnish
Brochel
Dun Caan
1,456 ft.

A896

Duirinish
MacLeod's
Tables

RAASAY

Inverarish

Howmore

The
Braes

Carbost
Sconser

SCALPAY

SOUTH
UIST

A863

Talisker

THE
CULLINS

Minginish

Kyleakin

A865

Daliburgh
Lochboisdale

car ferry to Lochboisdale

ISLE OF
SKYE

SOAY

Broadford

A851

Kylerhea

A87

Ludag

Elgol

Sleat

Eoligarry
ERISKAY

A'Chill

Cuillin Sound

Sound of Sleat

Borve
BARRA

Sound of Barra

CANNA

Kilmory

Sound of Canna

Armadale
Ardvasar

VATERSAY
SANDRAY

Castlebay

RUM
Kinloch

Mallaig

Sound of
Mingulay
PABBAY

Sea
of the
Hebrides

Sound of Rum

EIGG

Glamisdale

A830

MINGULAY

Sound of Eigg

Port
Mor

A861

MUCK

0   15 miles

0   15 kilometers

Skye

Skye. Even the word itself sounds wildly romantic. So much has been written about this famous Hebridean island that sometimes one is at a loss to describe the island's incandescent beauty, its special aura. For when the light hits a certain way or a rainbow peeks fleetingly from behind swirling clouds, words are not enough.

Traditionally one came to Skye by sea. Nowadays though, contemporary travelers also have the option of driving across the controversial Skye Bridge (controversial because it costs almost £6 each way to cross it). While controversial, it is quite an engineering and aesthetic marvel, rising skyward from Kyle of Lochalsh to Kyleakin. For those who insist on catching a ferry to Skye, you can depart the traditional way from either Mallaig, Kylerhea, or the Western Isles.

The capital of Skye is Portree, a handsome town in which there is much to do. There are several fine restaurants ranging from Indian to vegetarian, as well as numerous craft and gift shops. Probably the most important attraction is the Aros Heritage Centre, which explores the island's tumultuous past. It also contains a fine restaurant and an excellent shop that stocks books and CDs. Gaelic concerts are held here during the summer months. Don't miss the An Tuireann Arts Centre, a combination art gallery and lovely café. Carmina Gadelica on Wentworth Street, Portree's main thoroughfare, is an excellent bookshop, especially strong on titles of local interest.

Skye has many faces. North of Portree, the Trotterish Peninsula offers some of the most spectacular scenery on the island, from the quiet beauty of the Old Man of Storr to the otherworldly rock formations of the Quiraing. Also in the vicinity, Flora MacDonald's grave and monument is located at Kilmuir. (MacDonald was the island heroine who saved Bonnie Prince Charlie's life back in 1745-46.) Duntulm Castle, now a ruin, was once the home of Clan MacDonald. The Museum of Island Life in the crofting township of Staffin is an outdoor living history museum of Skye heritage and customs, while the ferry port of Uig offers daily sailings to the Western Isles.

In western Skye, Dunvegan Castle, home to the chiefs of MacLeod for more than 700 years, has exhibits, gardens, craft shops, a restaurant, and even wildlife cruises. Northwest of Dunvegan, the MacCrimmon Piping Centre at Boreraig commemorates the wonderful gift that the MacCrimmons gave to the world—pibroch, the classical music of the Highland bagpipe. The museum is worth a visit, even for non-music-lovers.

Skye's southern peninsula, Sleat (pronounced "Slate"), is often called "The Garden of Skye," and for good reason. It is a lush area of woodland and greenery. The Clan Donald Visitor Centre houses the Museum of the Isles, which includes a restaurant, shop, and genealogy research library. Down the road from the center is Sabhal Mor Ostaig, Skye's Gaelic college and one of the leading institutions of the modern Gaelic cultural revival. Previously a farm that belonged to the MacDonalds (its name, in fact, translates into "big barn"), Sabhal Mor Ostaig offers short courses in Gaelic music, culture, and heritage.

There's much more to Skye than these few paragraphs suggest. One could spend a lifetime here exploring its corners and still not see everything.

Glenview Inn and Restaurant
Paul and Cathie Booth
Culnacnoc
By Staffin
Telephone: 01470-562248
Fax: 01470-562211
Bedrooms: 5 rooms; 4 ensuite, 1 with private bathroom.
Rates: From £25. **Credit cards:** VISA, MasterCard, Delta. **Open:** March-October. **Children:** Yes. **Pets:** Yes. **Smoking:** Restricted to residents lounge only. **Provision for handicapped:** No. **Directions:** Off the A855 on the Staffin Road, the Glenview Inn is located 12 miles north of Portree between the Old Man of Storr and the Quiraing.

One of the finest examples of traditional croft architecture, the Glenview Inn was built by a local merchant as a home and village shop. Today the old gentleman still remembers, according to Paul and Cathie Booth, bringing up the supplies landed by steamer from Glasgow in the bay below the inn. Tastefully modernized, this home away from home is located on the northern tip of Skye, in the Trotternish peninsula. Nearby are two of the island's eeriest rock formations, the Old Man of Storr and the Quiraing. Not surprisingly, walking, climbing, photography, and birdwatching are popular activities here. For quieter times, you can always enjoy the inn's peaceful sitting room, where you can nurse a local malt in front of the open fire or browse through their wide selection of books and maps. The evening meals are quite impressive, too: how about hot game haggis with rowanberry jelly and homemade oatcakes or Skye lobster tails sautéed in garlic butter for starters? For entrées consider the braised shank of Scottish lamb cooked Moroccan style with prunes, citrus fruit, and ginger and served on a bed of couscous. The next course could be a warm onion and pepper flan or a baked terrine of wild forest mushrooms with fresh tomatoes, mozzarella, herbs, and sweet potato baked with coconut milk and served with a leaf salad. If you have any room left for dessert, you can always choose between the bread and butter pudding, panna cotta with raspberry sauce, or hot apple and rhubarb pie with custard. For a lighter sendoff, try a plate of Scottish cheeses with biscuits, fruit, and celery. It's all scrumptious.

Flodigarry Country House Hotel
Pamela and Andrew Butler
Staffin
Telephone: 01470-552203
Fax: 01470-552301
Web site: www.milford.co.uk/scotland/accom/h-1-1741.html
Bedrooms: 19 rooms, all ensuite. (7 rooms in Flora's Cottage and 12 rooms in the main house.)
Rates: £49-75 pp. Main house: £49 B&B standard single, double, or twin; £75 dinner and B&B; superior double or twin £59 B&B, £85 dinner, B&B; flagship (Quiraing and Torridon) £75 B&B, £100 dinner, B&B. Flora MacDonald's Cottage: standard attic twin £49 B&B, £75 dinner, B&B; superior double or twin £59 B&B, £85 dinner, B&B.
Credit cards: VISA, MasterCard, Switch, Delta. **Open:** Year-round.
Children: No. **Pets:** Well-behaved dogs only, but not in public rooms—in the bedrooms and public bar only. **Smoking:** Allowed only in lounges and bar. **Provision for handicapped:** The ground floor bedroom in Flora's Cottage is designed with disabled guests in mind.
Directions: Located off the A855, about 20 miles north of Portree.

This grand old historic house offers great views over Flodigarry Island and across Staffin Bay to the Scottish mainland, accompanied by large doses of good old-fashioned Highland hospitality. Flodigarry is a small crofting village where Gaelic is still spoken. The hotel itself is surrounded by five acres of gardens and mixed woodland. A nineteenth-century mansion, Flodigarry was built as a private house in 1895 by Alexander Livingstone MacDonald on a site adjacent to the cottage where Flora MacDonald had once lived; it has been a hotel since 1928. The old billiard room has been converted into an attractive bar and a conservatory (outdoor terrace) with cast-iron pillars. The Water Horse Restaurant is cozy and intimate; four-course evening meals and traditional Sunday lunches are served here. The cottage next to the hotel was Flora and her family's home from 1751 to 1759; five of her seven children were born here. The cottage is tastefully renovated and consists of seven ensuite rooms, each uniquely decorated and furnished in period style—wooden olive-green chairs, targe (shield) above the bed, and a fireplace. A ruined broch, at least 500 years old, lies in the hotel garden. Watch out for golden eagles and otters along the seashore. Many fine coastal and hill walks are available from the hotel, including the Quiraing and Trotternish ridge walk. Sea fishing trips can also be arranged.

Lime Stone Cottage
Kathie M. McLoughlin
4 Lime Park
Broadford
Telephone: 01471-822142
Bedrooms: 3 rooms, all ensuite.
Rates: £18-25. **Credit cards:** None. **Open:** Year-round. **Children:** Yes.
Pets: No. **Smoking:** Restricted. **Provision for handicapped:** Restricted.
Directions: From the Skye Bridge take the A850 to Broadford. After passing the Claymore Restaurant, turn left into Lime Park. Turn right at the Reptile Centre. The cottage is 150 yards on your left.

This small turn-of-the-century crofter's cottage was originally built for workers at the local lime kiln. You can tell it dates from a different era and mindset—handsome and sturdy in a practical sort of way. Derelict for many years, it has been lovingly restored to retain its original character while still suiting the needs of modern travelers. It offers wonderful views over Broadford Bay to Loch Carron and the Scottish mainland. Kathie offers a comfortable sitting room with log fire for guests who have learned to appreciate the simple pleasures of life. She also serves a traditional home-cooked breakfast and caters to visitors with vegetarian or special diets. Packed lunches are available on request. Kathie is generous with advice when it comes to suggesting the many walks and tours offered on the island.

Whitewave Activities B&B
Anne Martin and John White
No. 19 Linicro
Kilmuir
By Portree
Telephone: 01470-542414
Fax: 01470-542443
E-mail: activities@whiteact.demon.co.uk
Web site: www.whiteact.demon.co.uk
Bedrooms: 6 rooms, 3 ensuite.
Rates: £16-17.50. **Credit cards:** VISA, MasterCard, Delta. **Open:** All year. **Children:** Very welcome; cot available. **Pets:** Very welcome. **Smoking:** No. **Provision for handicapped:** 1 family room (with double and single beds) with shared accessible shower facility and 1 twin room with ensuite accessible shower. **Directions:** Located just north of Uig, the ferry terminal for the Outer Hebrides. Follow signs to Uig, heading north on the A855, a single-track road that climbs out of Uig via a sharp hairpin bend.

Whitewave is a combination outdoor center, inn, ceilidh, and family home—certainly one of the most unusual places to stay on the island. Anne is a native Gaelic speaker as well as a professional Gaelic singer (her CD, "Co. . ?: Gaelic Song from the Isle of Skye," should be available from record shops in Portree or at the Aros Heritage Centre). "Being born and brought up in Skye I want our guests to leave with a real sense of having experienced the island through the activities they do, the music and Gaelic they hear, as well as enjoying good food and drink," she says. And not to forget, "our incredible sunsets." Whitewave offers many activities, including kayaking, windsurfing, archery, biking, cultural activities, and guided walks. Nearby is the Skye Museum of Island Life and the Kilmuir Cemetery, where Flora MacDonald is buried beneath an enormous Celtic cross.

Rosedale Hotel
The Andrew family
Beaumont Crescent
Portree
Telephone: 01478-613131
Fax: 01478-612531
Bedrooms: 23 rooms, all ensuite.
Rates: From £38. **Credit cards:** VISA. **Open:** Early May to mid-October.
Children: Yes. **Pets:** No. **Smoking:** Yes. **Provision for handicapped:** No.
Directions: Located on Portree's harbor front.

Located on the harborfront, the Rosedale is a row of whitewashed fisherman's cottages converted to a small hotel with views directly over the harbor. The staff is efficient and friendly, the rooms snug and warm. The restaurant has received several awards, and features a changing daily menu. The Rosedale has two very comfortable lounges that feature a fine selection of single malts. Of course, the fiery Talisker, Skye's single malt, is available at the bar. The Rosedale boasts a terrific location. Not only do you have the harbor, and indeed, the town of Portree, outside your door, but the rest of the island is also at your disposal. The Andrew family has run the hotel since the early 1950s, so they know what they're doing, and especially know how to please their customers, many of whom come back over and over again. A piece of advice: the interior consists of a labyrinth of hallways and doors, with no seeming order to them. Ask at the front desk if someone can escort you to your room, especially if you're carrying heavy luggage.

Kinloch Lodge
Lord and Lady Macdonald
Sleat
Telephone: 01471-833214
Fax: 01471-833277
E-mail: kinloch@dial.pipex.com
Web sites: www.kinloch-lodge.co.uk; www.claire-macdonald.com
Bedrooms: 10 rooms, all ensuite in Kinloch Lodge; 5 rooms, all ensuite in Kinloch.
Rates: £38-95 (Kinloch Lodge); £58-95 Kinloch (The New House).
Credit cards: MasterCard/Eurocard, American Express, VISA, Access.
Open: Year-round except Christmas. **Children:** Yes. **Pets:** By arrangement. **Smoking:** Not in bedrooms or dining room. **Provision for handicapped:** No. **Directions:** 8 miles south of Broadford on the A851; 10 miles north of Armadale on A851. From the Skye Bridge turn right at the roundabout leading to Portree. Follow the A87 for 5 miles, then turn left onto the A851 to Armadale. The turnoff to Kinloch Lodge is 5 miles down the road on the left. Follow the small road for about a mile. From Armadale Ferry take the A851 to Isle Ornsay and Broadford. Kinloch Lodge is 10 miles north on the right-hand side of the road.

Staying at Kinloch Lodge is truly a memorable experience. From the gracious staff to the sumptuous meals, Kinloch represents the finest in Scottish hospitality. Secluded between a wooded hillside and the sea loch on two sides, Kinloch is the ancestral home of Lord Macdonald of Macdonald, High Chief of Clan Donald. He and his writer wife Claire Macdonald have run it as a small, personally run hotel for nearly 30 years. This handsome white-painted country house hotel dates back to the early 1600s, when it was built as a farmhouse, which later expanded to a sporting lodge in the nineteenth century. The subtly elegant décor reflects Lady Claire MacDonald's taste—long mirrors, old family portraits on dark green walls, and antiques. Lady Claire, an award-winning journalist and author of more than a dozen best-selling cookbooks, presents a five-course menu each night. Don't be put off by it all, though. Claire is thoroughly down to earth and very funny. She possesses that special gift that allows people to feel instantly at home—no matter how elaborate the circumstances. Guests help themselves to drinks in the drawing room before dinner, which is served about 8 P.M. The menu changes daily. Typically you have a choice of two first courses (always fish or shellfish), soup, and choice of two main courses, followed by a choice of two puddings. Cheese, biscuits, and fresh fruit are on the sideboard for guests to help themselves. The daily menu is placed in each bedroom with the wine list; guests are asked to list their room number and their choices by afternoon or early evening. In 1998 the Macdonalds built a new addition, Kinloch, which is adjacent to the Lodge. Guests staying in Kinloch have breakfast and dinner in the Lodge. Pre-dinner drinks and after-dinner coffee and fudge can be enjoyed in Kinloch's drawing room. In addition to five more rooms, Kinloch also houses the Claire Macdonald Centre for Food and Taste, perfect for those with deep pockets who love to cook. The center offers an annual program of cooking demonstrations, which are limited to about 20 people. Prices range from £300-350 per person and include three nights' dinner, bed and breakfast, and light lunch, with two full mornings of demonstrations.

Hotel Eilean Iarmain (Isle Ornsay Hotel)
Sir Iain and Lady Noble
Isle Ornsay
Sleat
Telephone: 01471-833332
Fax: 01471-833275
Bedrooms: 12 rooms, all ensuite (6 in the Garden House and 6 in the main hotel).
Rates: £55 double. **Credit cards:** Access, VISA, American Express, Delta, Switch. **Open:** Year-round. **Children:** Yes. **Pets:** Well-behaved pets only by private arrangement. **Smoking:** Some bedrooms are non-smoking. **Provision for handicapped:** Yes. **Directions:** From Mallaig/Armadale ferry turn right onto the A852,then right again at the sign for Isle Ornsay. The hotel is located at the water's edge.

This small whitewashed hotel was built in 1888 and stands on a small bay of Isle Ornsay, on the south peninsula of Skye. It's a tranquil place, with log fires and dinner by candlelight. The rooms are decorated with original features and period furniture. One room has a half tester canopy bed from nearby Armadale Castle, draped in pretty fabrics. Small touches add considerably to the genial atmosphere, such as complimentary tea, coffee, chocolate, shortbread, hair dryer, toiletries, and robes. The hotel is owned by Sir Iain Noble, a controversial figure in these parts, who has been a vigorous supporter of Gaelic culture for many years (too aggressive for some islander's tastes, as it turns out). Many of the staff members are Gaelic speakers. All rooms also have on hand samples of Te Bheag whisky. Established by Iain Noble in 1976 to supply the Hebrides, the headquarters of the Gaelic Whiskies (Praban Na Linne) are based at Eilean Iarmain, the only whisky company with its home in Skye. The food at the hotel is fresh. Game and venison comes from their own estate, and shellfish is taken straight from the old stone pier just yards from the hotel. Traditional afternoon teas are served every day. The Nobles have recently added several new suites. There is also a small sitting room downstairs. One of the upstairs bedrooms overlooks a view of sea and hills and the lighthouse built by Robert Louis Stevenson's grandfather.

ALSO RECOMMENDED

Dunvegan, *The Tables Hotel & Restaurant.* Telephone: 01470-521404. Fax: 01470-521404. 5 rooms, 4 ensuite. Overlooking Loch Dunvegan and MacLeod's Tables. Located one mile from Dunvegan Castle, Dunvegan contains an award-winning restaurant, a fine selection of good wines and single malts, and a warm peat fire.

Glen Eynort, *The Blue Lobster,* Robert J. Van der Vliet, Glen Eynort. Telephone: 01478-640320. 3 rooms. Charming little cottage by Carbost.

Kilmuir, *Kilmuir House,* Mrs. S. C. Phelps, near Uig. Telephone: 01470-542262. Fax: 01470-542461. E-mail: phelpskilmuirhouseskye@btinternet.com. 3 rooms. Lovely old manse in walled garden overlooking Loch Snizort. Decorated with antiques. Mrs. Phelps uses local produce and her own free-range eggs. Kilmuir is the ideal area for birdwatchers, as well as a great place to check out the fabulous sunsets.

Portree, *The Pink Guest House,* 1 Quay Street. Telephone: 01478-612263. Fax: 01478-612181. 9 rooms, 7 ensuite. Lovely accommodation on Portree Harbor.

Sleat, *The Collies,* Patricia Phillips, 4 Camus Cross, Isle Ornsay. Telephone: 01471-833237. 2 rooms. A non-smoking house, the Collies is located in a quiet area overlooking Isle Ornsay Bay. Breakfast includes fresh eggs from the croft and homemade jams.

Talisker, *Talisker House.* Telephone: 01478-640245. Fax: 01478-640214. E-mail: jon_and_ros.wathen@virgin.net. Web site: www.host.co.uk. 4 rooms, all ensuite. Country house on Skye's west coast. Boswell and Johnson visited in 1773. Features spacious rooms and leisurely dinners.

Treaslane, *Auchendinny Guest House,* Ann and Derek Howes, by Portree. Telephone: 01470-532470. Fax: 01470-532470. 7 rooms, all ensuite. Offers wonderful views of the Aird and Trotternish Hills, as well as comfy accommodations. Choice of full, cooked, or continental breakfasts. Vegetarian dishes available on request. Located just off the Portree to Dunvegan Road, beside a tidal loch; hence, the bird life and frolicking seals provide guaranteed free entertainment.

Western Isles

The Western Isles includes Lewis, Harris, North and South Uist, Barra, and Benbecula, a 130-mile long chain of islands northwest of the Scottish mainland. Perhaps it is their very remoteness that has captured the imagination of writers, artists, and travelers for centuries.

Lewis and Harris form one island: Lewis in the north and Harris in the south. The population of Lewis is about 20,000, Harris only 2,200.

Lewis is largely rolling moorland and gentle hills along with countless lochs and lochans. The western and eastern coasts tend to be more mountainous, with exposed cliffs hanging over rocky shores. Stornoway, the only real town on the island, contains the premier arts venue in the Western Isles. An Lanntair in the Town Hall along South Beach opened in 1985 and hosts exhibitions, concerts, and theater presentations. It also houses an attractive café.

Some of the most important prehistoric landmarks are located in Lewis. The best-known is undoubtedly Callanish, or Calanais, the five-thousand-year-old standing stones that are just as impressive as Stonehenge, perhaps more so, for at least up here you can actually get close to the stones.

Harris is an indescribably beautiful island, offering a breathtaking landscape of mountains, lochs, and peatlands. The island is best known for Harris Tweed, even though it is made on both Harris and Lewis. Note: in order for it to be authentic Harris Tweed it must bear the orb symbol, the mark of the Harris Tweed Association. The lunar landscape and fjord-like lochs of South Harris give way to the gloriously white and clean sandy beaches of Southwest Harris. It is difficult to describe the feeling you get after seeing these usually empty beaches for the first time. They literally take your breath away. A big part of their appeal, of course, is the surprise factor. Who would have thought it possible to see beaches as beautiful as anything in the Mediterranean or other warm-weather climates this far north? Harris is like that, though. It is full of surprises.

Yet each of the islands retains its own particular beauty. Each has something special to offer the visitor who dares to travel this far off the beaten path.

LEWIS

Eshcol Guest House
Neil and Isobel Macarthur
Breasclete
Callanish
Isle of Lewis
Telephone/Fax: 01851-621357
Bedrooms: 3 rooms, 2 ensuite.
Rates: £30. **Credit cards**: None. **Open**: Closed Christmas and New
Year's. **Children**: Over 8. **Pets**: By arrangement. **Smoking**: No.
Provision for handicapped: No. **Directions**: From Stornoway take the
A859 south for 8 miles. At Levebost turn right and take the A858 an
additional 10 miles to Breasclete.

This modern guesthouse is located on a small croft in the small
weaving village of Breasclete, on the west coast of Lewis. Quality and
service are its calling cards. And since it is situated only two miles from
the famous Callanish Standing Stones, and three miles from the
Carlaway Broch, it is the perfect location for those visitors who wish
to explore in-depth the many ancient sites in this area of Lewis, as well
as nearby Harris. Your hosts were born and bred in the village of
Breasclete and possess considerable knowledge about the area and
its history. Neil himself is a native Gaelic speaker. The otherworldly
views from the lounge across Loch Roag to Great Bernera are worth
the journey alone. The three bedrooms are tastefully decorated. The
Macarthurs offer home cooking using produce from their own veg-
etable garden (in season). It's been said by more than a few visitors
that Neil makes the best porridge in Scotland. The Macarthurs would
be happy to arrange a local rental car to meet you at the airport or
the ferry terminal on request.

Park Guest House
Roddy and Catherine Afrin
30 James Street
Stornoway
Isle of Lewis
Telephone: 01851-702485 or 01851-703482
Fax: 01851-703482
Bedrooms: 8 rooms, 3 ensuite.
Rates: From £32 pp (ensuite). **Credit cards**: MasterCard/Eurocard, VISA, Delta. **Open**: Year-round except Christmas Eve to January 5. **Children**: Yes. **Pets**: No. **Smoking**: Yes. **Provision for handicapped**: Yes. **Directions**: Turn left off the the ferry terminal, then left into Shell Street. Make a right at the first roundabou into James Street. The guesthouse is 200 yards on the left.

Built in 1883, this handsome stone-built Victorian townhouse offers some of the finest and most reasonable accommodations in Stornoway. Both the staff and the management are uniformly friendly and extremely helpful. The owners, Roddy and Catherine Afrin, come from interesting backgrounds. Catherine studied at the Glasgow School of Art, while the youthful and energetic Roddy (usually dressed in a casual white T-shirt) was a former head chef on an oil rig in the North Sea. He selects and prepares the locally produced food, much of it consisting of fresh fish from local fishing boats, as well as local lamb and venison. Dinners can consist of dishes such as venison soup, local prawns, lobster, salmon, and island-grown lamb. Meals are handsomely presented. Look for Stornoway black pudding (blood sausage) at the breakfast table, along with other hearty fare. The

Victorian-era atmosphere is faithfully captured, from the careful restoration of the original woodwork to the attention to detail applied to the bedrooms and public areas. The comfortable sitting room boasts a well-stocked bookshelf. Within walking distance is the harbor, the library with its extensive local history section, and the Museum nan Eilean, a local history museum that explores the area's rich Gaelic culture and heritage. In addition, the sports center is only yards away, and a full 18-hole golf course is located within the grounds of nearby Lews Castle. The grounds are a lovely place to do a leisurely stroll and admire the trees and rhododendrons planted by Lewis's original owners, Sir James and Lady Matheson.

Ravenswood
Anne MacLeod
12 Matheson Road
Stornoway
Isle of Lewis
Telephone/Fax: 01851-702673
Bedrooms: 3 rooms, 2 ensuite.
Rates: £20-25. **Credit cards**: None. **Open**: Year-round except two weeks in October and 2 weeks at Christmas and New Year's. **Children**: Yes. **Pets**: No. **Smoking**: No. **Provision for handicapped**: No. **Directions**: From Stornoway ferry terminal turn left onto the main road to the mini-roundabout. Turn right onto James Street and proceed to a second mini-round. Turn left onto Matheson Road. Ravenswood is on the left-hand side.

This detached Victorian villa, built in 1901, is located on leafy Matheson Road, in a quiet section of Stornoway that is far removed from the commotion of the town center. (I highly recommend that you avoid the busy streets of the town center on weekends when the island's young people descend on Stornoway.) Matheson Road is named after Lady Matheson, whose husband Sir James Matheson purchased Lewis in 1844. Mrs. MacLeod, the present owner, tastefully upgraded her home in 1992. It offers a spacious sitting and dining room, attractive and clean rooms, and a relaxing atmosphere. It is also within walking distance of Stornoway's major sites.

ISLE OF HARRIS

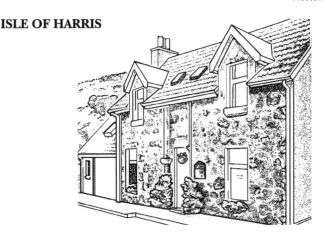

Allan Cottage Guest House
Bill and Evelyn Reed
The Old Telephone Exchange
Tarbert
Telephone/Fax: 01859-502146
Web site: www.witb.co.uk/links/allancottage.htm
Bedrooms: 3 rooms, 2 ensuite.
Rates: £30-35 double; with dinner, £55-60. **Credit cards:** None. **Open:** May 1-September 30. **Children:** Over 10 years. **Pets:** Yes. **Smoking:** In lounge only. **Provision for handicapped:** No. **Directions:** From the ferry terminal turn left, then make a hard first right turn onto the main village street.

Formerly the telephone exchange for the Isle of Harris, Allan Cottage is a small traditional country house of unusual charm and character. It stands at the end of the village of Tarbert, looking across the Minch toward the mountains of Skye. The nearby Shiant Islands shelter a colony of puffins, those comical-looking little birds that are so common in northern waters. The dining room is furnished with antiques, and the cozy lounge boasts an open fire, comfy armchairs, and books of local interest. Excellent cuisine is prepared by Bill, the chef/proprietor extraordinaire who, he says, "regards each evening meal as a small dinner party. We feel that by offering comfortable accommodation and first-class food to a small number of guests we are able to give a truly personal service." While here, do take the time to visit the immediate vicinity. Tarbert, for example, is the "capital" of Harris. With a population of about 500, the village was established as a fishing community back in 1779. A lovely tearoom, First Fruits, is located next to the tourist office.

Scarista House
Ian and Jane Callaghan
Scarista
Isle of Harris
Telephone: 01859-550238
Fax: 01859-550277
E-mail: ian@scaristahouse.demon.co.uk
Web site: www.scaristahouse.demon.co.uk
Bedrooms: 5 rooms, all ensuite.
Rates: £58 pp. **Credit cards**: MasterCard/Eurocard, VISA. **Open**: May-September. **Children**: Over 8. **Smoking**: In annex only. **Pets**: In annex only. **Provision for handicapped**: No. **Directions**: 15 minutes southwest of Tarbert on A859.

Scarista House, probably one of the most famous lodgings in all of Scotland, boasts a fascinating history. The original owners, Aberdeen-bred Alison Johnson and her husband Andrew, converted a derelict old manse, formerly the residence of the local Church of Scotland minister and one of the few landmark buildings in the Western Isles, into a highly acclaimed hotel. Although they sold the hotel in 1989, the often-hilarious story of their hard-earned triumphs and frequent struggles makes for good reading (you can pick up a copy of Alison's *A House By the Shore* at most bookstores throughout Scotland). Today the current owners, Ian and Jane Callaghan, have taken up the torch. Their quiet country guesthouse retains its spectacular location overlooking a three-mile shell-sand beach. All rooms offer excellent views over the garden to the sea beyond. Their library stocks a large collection of books, including many of local interest, for browsing and glows with an open fire. They also make available to their guests record and CD players, but no newspapers, television, or radio (after all, you didn't come all the way to Harris to keep up with the rest of the world, did you?). Like their predecessors, the Callaghans serve mainly organic produce, with lots of local fish and shellfish in a menu that changes daily, as well as fresh vegetables and herbs from the garden. Your morning eggs are from their own hens. Breakfasts usually consist of fruit juice, fresh fruit salad, black pudding, kippers and herring, and fine teas and coffees. All of their breads, cakes, and biscuits are homemade, as is their marmalade and yogurt. A candlelit dinner is served in the evening, using silver tableware and fine china. There is a solid wine list, too. All in all, Scarista is a special kind of place.

St. Kilda House
Sue Massey and Jim Shaw
Leverburgh
Isle of Harris
Telephone: 01859-520419
Bedrooms: 2 rooms; 1 twin and 1 double.
Rates: £20-25 pp for 5-course evening meal. **Credit cards**: None. **Open**: Year-round. **Children**: Yes. **Pets**: No. **Smoking**: No. **Provision for handicapped**: No. **Directions**: From Tarbert go south towards Leverburgh (in Gaelic, An-T-Ob). On reaching Leverburgh, follow the road until you come to a right turn marked "Uist car ferry," then turn right and follow that road until you come to a left turn marked "Strond." Turn left onto this road. St. Kilda is the fifth house on the left.

St. Kilda was Leverburgh's schoolhouse from 1887 to 1932, and even today there is a strong sense of history about it. Like many places on Harris, it offers impressive views, from the rolling hills from the rear of the house to the equally spectacular views across the Sound of Harris from the front. Sue and Jim, who set up shop here in the early 1990s, present a varied breakfast menu as well as a five-course evening meal. They are known for their homemade bread. The rooms are extremely comfortable; one offers a dead-gorgeous sea view. Nearby are plenty of opportunities for fishing, sailing, nine-hole golfing, hill-walking, and birdwatching. Packed lunches are available upon request.

ALSO RECOMMENDED

Castlebay, *Tigh-na-Mara,* Linda and Archie Maclean, Isle of Barra. Telephone: 01871-810304. 5 rooms, all ensuite. Comfortable old stone building offering both breakfast and evening meals.

Lochmaddy, *The Old Courthouse,* Margaret Johnson, North Uist. Telephone: 01876-500358. 4 rooms, all ensuite. In an earlier life this colorful B&B functioned as both courthouse and jail for all of the Western Isles. Gaelic is spoken here. Mrs. Johnson has earned a reputation as an excellent cook, including her vegetarian meals. The visitor center, Taigh Chearsahagh, located near the pier, is a combination local history museum, art gallery, shop, and café.

Isle of Harris, *Carminish Guest House,* Mary and Alex Borthwick, 1A Strond. Telephone: 01859-520400. 3 rooms, all ensuite. Spacious house situated on the Strong/Barrosdale Road, secluded with hills on one side and facing the sea on the other. The nearest neighbors are a half mile on either side. A five-course dinner is available in the evenings.

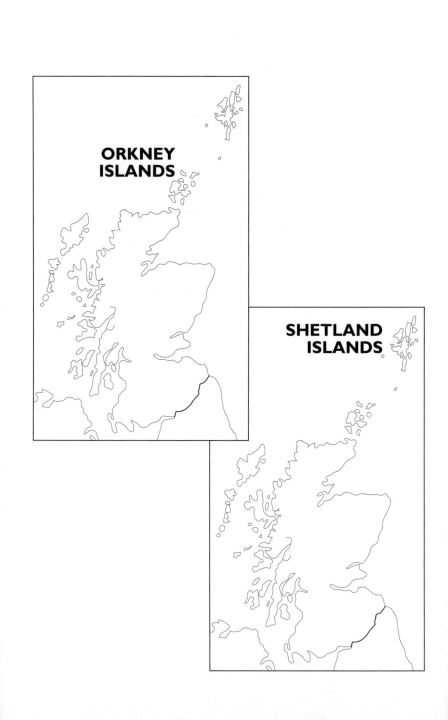

ORKNEY ISLANDS

SHETLAND ISLANDS

Orkney & Shetland

North of the Scottish mainland lies a chain of islands that appears more Scandinavian than Scottish. The lilt of their singsong accent reminds one of Norway. The place-names are largely Scandinavian, as are the island folklore and legends, and even the fiddling tradition smacks of Scandinavian rhythms and scales.

Other images linger in the mind's eye: long summer nights, pre-historic standing stones, the warm glow emanating from St. Magnus' Cathedral, and a Viking boat in Lerwick harbor.

Orkney consists of about 70 islands, most of them green, fertile, and flat. Kirkwall, the capital, is home to the prestigious St. Magnus Festival, a major arts fest held each June and one of the finest in Britain. Many of the concerts and musical events take place in the breathtakingly beautiful St. Magnus Cathedral. Stromness is irre-sistibly gorgeous, a picture-postcard town of neat stone houses on narrow winding lanes that tumble down to the sea, sort of an Orcadian version of Dylan Thomas's fictitious Welsh village of Llareggub. One sometimes forgets that places like this really do exist.

Beyond the towns themselves are numerous prehistoric sites scat-tered throughout the islands: the Stone Age village of Skara Brae, the Neolithic burial chamber of Maes Howe, the Standing Stones of Stenness, and the Ring of Brodgar. All remind us just how long these far-away islands have been populated.

About 60 miles north of Orkney is Shetland. These 100 or so islands are considerably rougher and wilder, and more mountainous, than their gentler neighbor to the south.

Lerwick is the commercial capital of Shetland, a small big town of about 7,500 people that is still enjoying the prosperity that has arrived with the North Sea oil boom. The Shetland Room in the Shetland Library and Museum harbors a vast collection of local literature.

Around Shetland don't miss the magnificent Mousa Broch, an impressive fortress that stood guard on the tiny island of Mousa for

2,000 years. It is considered the best-preserved fortress in Scotland. Meanwhile, at the southern tip of mainland Shetland, at Sumburgh Head, is another equally impressive historic monument. Jarlshof was continuously occupied for more than 4,000 years; the buildings range from Norse long house to medieval farmstead.

Lav'rockha Guest House
John D. Webster
Inganess Road
St. Ola
Kirkwall
Orkney
Telephone/Fax: 01856-876103
E-mail: lavrockha@orkney.com
Web site: www.norsecom.co.uk/lavrockha
Bedrooms: 5 rooms, all ensuite.
Rates: £18-27. **Credit cards:** VISA, MasterCard, Delta. **Open:** Year-round. **Children:** Well-behaved children only. There is a £6 charge for children ages two to twelve years, sharing with adults; children under age two stay free. **Pets:** Guide dogs only. **Smoking:** No. **Provision for handicapped:** Unassisted wheelchair access. Wheelchair-friendly entrance and ground floor. **Directions:** Five minutes from Kirkwall Airport. On entering town, Inganess Road is the first road on the right. The guesthouse is located about 100 meters on the right.

Convenient to the airport, ferries to the northern isles, and other forms of transport, Lav'rocka offers comfortable accommodations at affordable rates. It's less than a mile from the town center and a short walk from Highland Park Distillery & Visitor Centre, the northern-most distillery in Scotland. Mr. Webster runs a simple and clean home, with no pretensions. The private resident's lounge has both television and video player, while business guests have access to both fax and e-mail services. In addition, the enclosed outdoor play area is ideal for children.

Stoneyquoy Farm B&B
Louise and Arthur Budge
Lyness
Isle of Hoy
Orkney
Telephone/Fax: 01856-791234
Web site: www.orknet.co.uk/tourism/hoy.htm
Bedrooms: 2 rooms, both ensuite.
Rates: £18. **Credit cards:** None. **Open:** All year. **Children:** Yes. **Pets:** No. **Smoking:** No. **Provision for handicapped:** No. **Directions:** From Orkney's Houton pier take the ferry to Lyness on the island of Hoy. Drive three miles towards Longhope. The farm is on the right side.

This nicely appointed farmhouse and 200-acre beef farm offers an interesting mix of Orcadian and Dutch hospitality. Arthur, a native Orcadian, took over the farm from his parents in 1974. Louise is Dutch and came to Scotland as a tourist about 25 years ago and has been here ever since. A member of the Orkney Tourist Guides Association, she offers personally guided tours of Hoy and the islands, and can answer most any question put to her about Orkney. The house is furnished with antiques, Orkney chairs (a distinctive type of high-backed chair manufactured in Orkney), an open fire in the sitting room, and many reading materials, as well as board games, a music center, and television. Louise and Arthur often invite guests to join them on evening walks to view their cattle. For evening meals Louise prefers to use Orkney produce whenever possible (soup is her specialty), and serves Dutch coffee after dinner. Hoy is Orkney's largest outer island (about 26 miles long by 5 miles wide), with a population of only 450.

ALSO RECOMMENDED

Brae, *Busta House Hotel,* Peter and Judith Jones, Busta, Shetland. Telephone: 01806-522506. Fax: 01806-522588. E-mail: busta@mes.co.uk. Website: www.mes.co.uk/busta. 20 rooms, all ensuite. Historic home with great views set in a sixteenth-century laird's house complete with walled gardens and private piers.

Lerwick, *Glen Orchy Guest House,* Joan and Trevor Howarth, 20 Knab Road, Shetland. Telephone/Fax: 01595-692031. 14 rooms, all ensuite. This quiet B&B on the south side of Lerwick is located near the town center and a short distance from a nine-hole golf course.

Lerwick, *Knysa Guest House,* 6 Burgh Road. Telephone: 01595-694865. 4 rooms. Offering friendly service and hearty breakfasts, this substantially built home is located in a quiet residential section of town, a short walk from the town center.

Orphir, *Chinegar,* Mr. and Mrs. Wallington, Orkney. Telephone: 01856-811236. 1 room. Working croft located midway between Kirkwall and Stromness, overlooking Scapa Flow. Includes an artist's studio and the warm glow of a peat fire. Nearby is the Round Kirk, Scotland's only circular medieval church, which stands next to Earl's Bu, a Viking drinking hall. You can learn more about the Norse roots of Orkney and its wonderful collection of Viking tales at the Orkneyinga Saga Experience, a new interpretation center.

St. Margaret's Hope, *Creel Restaurant & Rooms,* Joyce and Alan Craigie, Front Road, South Ronaldsay, Orkney. Telephone: 01856-831311. 3 rooms, all ensuite. This small family-run and highly acclaimed seafront restaurant, whitewashed and gabled, provides truly innovative modern cooking, although traditional Orcadian influences, such as Orcadian crab soup, are not overlooked either. The excellent though limited menu changes daily according to availability. Two of the spacious rooms offer sea views.

Stenness, *The Mill of Eyrland,* Orkney. Telephone: 01856-850136. Fax: 01856-851633. E-mail: kenandmorag@millofeyrland.demon.co.uk. Web site: www.orknet.co.uk/mill. 3 rooms, 2 ensuite. Converted mill set amid lovely gardens located only three miles from Stromness. Built in 1861, the mill served the Stenness and Orphir communities for more than a century. Stay here and you'll know that it's no typical B&B.

Index

LODGINGS

TRAVEL NOTES

TRAVEL NOTES

TRAVEL NOTES

TRAVEL NOTES

TRAVEL NOTES